CHRISTIAN POEMS, SPEECHES & SKITS FOR EASTER AND CHRISTMAS PROGRAMS

Pearl Robinson

WESTBOW
PRESS®
A DIVISION OF THOMAS NELSON
& ZONDERVAN

WestBow Press books may be ordered through booksellers or by contacting:

WestBow Press
A Division of Thomas Nelson & Zondervan
1663 Liberty Drive
Bloomington, IN 47403
www.westbowpress.com
844-714-3454

Scripture quotations are taken from the New King James Version®. Copyright © 1982 by Thomas Nelson. Used by permission. All rights reserved.

ISBN: 978-1-9736-9942-2 (sc)
ISBN: 978-1-9736-9886-9 (e)

Library of Congress Control Number: 2023909848

Print information available on the last page.

WestBow Press rev. date: 8/25/2023

DEDICATION

I dedicate this book to Jesus Christ, my Lord and Savior.
To my sons, Jimmy (and his wife, Deanna) and Jamel. To
my five loving grandchildren: Antonishe, Nijana, Malachi,
Avery, and Sanai. To my sisters Annie, Shirley, Mary,
Ruthie, and Maggie. And to my loving husband Robby, who
supported me throughout writing this book in 2005.

CONTENTS

Preface xiii

Introduction xv

For Resurrection Day 1

    He Loves Me 3
    Christ Died 4
    My Savior 5
    I am Free. 6
    Jesus, you were brave. 7
    He Lives. 8
    Thanks 9
    Lots of love 10
    I Understand 11
    Loving You 12
    Where Is Jesus? 13
    A Second Chance 14
    Christ Makes Me Glad 15
    He Never Complained 16
    My Hero 17
    He Will Return 18
    Christ died on the Cross. 19
    My Blessing 20
    I Am Ready 21
    He Left Me 22

Obey Him.. 23

On the Cross 24

Innocent Blood Shed.. 25

Easter Time 26

Christ Is in Heaven 27

Easter Thanks 28

Let His Light Shine 29

Beaten 30

Why for Me? 31

Christ, Please Don't Die 32

My Friend 33

Things I Will Do for Christ 34

Today I Feel Blessed.. 35

I Honor You... 36

An Empty Tomb... 37

Up Calvary's Hill.. 38

He Carried His Cross 39

Today Christ Lives... 40

Bound in Chains.. 41

Christ, Wait, I will Go with You. 42

Christ, Can You Walk with Me?............................... 43

Jesus Christ 44

Christ Died for Me.. 45

Christ Lives in My Heart 46

Nailed to the Cross 47

Resurrection Joy.. 48

Easter Day.. 49

Easter Songs 50

He Gave His Life 51

If Christ Had Not Died.. 52

Forgive Me, Christ 53

Where Would I Be? 54

They Crucified My Son 55

Christ Resurrected 56

I Will Honor and Praise You, Christ........................ 57

He Is Coming Back 58

My Thanks to Christ 59

A Letter to Christ 60

Thanks to God the Father 61

Welcome to the Program 62

A Resurrection Day Program Prayer 63

Christmas Program 65

Born to Die 67

Hail to the King 68

Christ Makes Me Smile 69

Thanks to God 70

Who Is This Baby? 71

God's Only Son 72

I Will 73

He Brought Joy 74

Baby Jesus 75

Lots of Love 76

Holy and Divine 77

Christ's Birth Makes Me Happy 78

My Blessing 79

I Am Ready 80

He Left Me 81

Christmas, a Time to Share 82

Welcome 83

Who Is this Baby Jesus? 84

I Love You, Christ 85

One Who Was Blessed 86

A Silent Night 87

A Time for Giving 88

A Holy Night 89

Born to Save All 90

Merry Christmas 91

A King Was Born 92

The Greatest Gift 93

Born without Sin 94

Christ, You Can Have My Bed 95

Hated by Many; Loved by Few 96

Hated by the King 97

A Holy Baby 98

Let Us Worship this Baby. 99

The Greatest Gift 100

An Amazing Birth 101

The Promise Savior Has Come 102

Bound by Sin 103

Thank You for Coming 104

Christmastime 105

Miracle Baby 106

Let Us Worship this Baby. 107

No Place to Call Home 108

A Baby, a Savior 109

Christmas Memories 110

A Gift from Heaven 111

Jesus Loves the Lost 112

Born in a Stable 113

Born to Die for You and Me 114

Underneath the Stars 115

Follow that Star. 116

Thank You, God 117

Welcome 118

A Christmas Prayer 119

Christmas and Resurrection Day Skits 121

A Walk to the Crucifixion 123

I Must Die 127

We Can Save Christ; I Know We Can 131

We Must Tell the Good News 134

A Free Gift 138

Come and Let us Worship the Baby. 141

A Christmas Skit, Jesus Is the Reason for The Season! 145

More Poems and Speeches...149

    Watched from Above 151
    Jesus Is All You Need for Christmas 152
    Christmas Thoughts...153
    A Precious Gift 154
    Mary, Mother of Jesus...155
    Joseph, a Wise Man 156
    An Innocent Baby...157
    Welcome His Birth 159
    Jesus Came to Give Us Hope 160
    Jesus Is Waiting..161
    Mary's Savior Too 162
    King Jesus 163
    A Talk with Christ... 164
    If You Love Christ, Share the Good News 165
    A Place Not Fit for a King 166
    Hallelujah 167
    He Is Coming Back 168
    My Thanks to Christ 169
    A Mother's Love 170
    Christ Is Alive and Waiting for You..................................171
    Mary's Broken Heart 172
    Things Christ May Have Said to His Father 173
    Jesus Is with Me 174
    Christ, Can You Walk with Me?.......................................175
    Christ's Walk to the Cross 176
    Christ's Thoughts on the Cross.. 177
    He Came Back to Life...178
    If I Could Have Carried His Cross 179
    Christ Obeyed His Father 180
    Peace, Love, and Joy..181
    I Watched, and I Listened...182
    Christ Will Return 183
    Stop Beating Him.. 184
    Christ Is Always with Me...185

I Wish 186

Can I See Your Hands? 187

He Is All You Need 188

Pride 189

Pray in Jesus' Name 190

He Listens 191

I Will Follow You Forever 192

There Is Joy in Knowing Christ 193

Christ Is 194

A Play 195

The Play 227

It Touched My Heart (A True Story) 265

Father, Please Bless this Book 267

PREFACE

This book aims to teach everyone who reads or hears the skits, speeches, and poems that Jesus is the reason for celebrating Easter and Christmas. Easter is the Resurrection Day when Jesus arose after being crucified. Christmas is a time of year when we celebrate the birth of our Lord and Savior. He was born to be a sacrifice to save the world.

I want children to learn about Jesus at an early age; therefore, you will find poems for children as young as two. Children will be excited to have an Easter speech to learn. I wrote some speeches and poems in the past tense. I did it because I wanted the children to act out the poems in drama. Leaders, please be creative and perhaps have the children say Happy Resurrection Day at the end of each speech. They can have fun and understand the seriousness of what Jesus Christ did for them.

I remember when I was a little girl. Easter and Christmas were exciting for me. I wanted to recreate a traditional Easter book for children today to learn about Jesus. The church would purchase a book that was full of Easter speeches. A speech was then cut from the book and given to each child. My mother made sure we would learn to recite our speech. Every poem and skit represent Jesus. The primary purpose of this book is I want all who read and hear the content in this book to accept Jesus as Lord and Savior.

INTRODUCTION

You will find a traditional Easter and Christmas program in this book. There are poems for children as young as two and youth. There are skits where children will learn the plan of Salvation. You will discover that Jesus is alive after dying for the sins of the world.

A children's ministry leader can create a program for the congregation to enjoy as the children teach them about our Lord and Savior, Jesus Christ. This book is also perfect for parents to read to their children, teaching them why God sent His only son to be born in a cruel and evil world.

You will also find two plays, Resurrection Day and Christmas Play. These two dramas will teach all the true meaning of celebrating Christmas and Easter.

I believe many who will read and hear the content of this book will accept Jesus as their Savior and make Him the Lord of their lives.

For Resurrection Day

HE LOVES ME

Jesus loves me.
I know this for sure.
He took my sins to the cross
Now I am free.

CHRIST DIED

I am happy
as I can be.
Christ died
for you and me.

MY SAVIOR

Jesus is my Savior.
Because He cares.
Is He yours?
If not, I will share.

I AM FREE.

I am not sad.
I am not mad.
Today I am glad.
Christ died for me.
Now I am free.

JESUS, YOU WERE BRAVE.

You carried your cross.
You did not give up.
You were tough.
You were brave.
Today I am not lost.
I am saved.

HE LIVES

Jesus is alive.
How do I know?
He lives in my heart.

THANKS

I give thanks to Jesus.
You have done so much.
You died on the cross for me.
And you arose on the third day.
Jesus, thanks a bunch.

LOTS OF LOVE

I have Lots of love.
To give to Jesus
Because He first loved me.

I UNDERSTAND

Jesus, I understand
why you died for me.
Now I am the happiest girl,
in the entire world.

LOVING YOU

Christ, loving you.
Makes me so happy.
Loving you, Christ,
is how I want to
live my life.

WHERE IS JESUS?

Jesus lives in my heart.
He is also in Heaven.
He watches over me.
He loves me, can't you see?

A SECOND CHANCE

When I heard Jesus was nailed and died on the cross,
I knew He gave me a second chance.
To live my life free of sin
If I am willing to open my heart,
and let Christ in; I would have a new start.

CHRIST MAKES ME GLAD

When my friends make me sad
And my teacher says I am acting bad,
I can always depend on Christ,
because He makes me glad.

HE NEVER COMPLAINED

Jesus Christ is a strong man.
The soldiers beat Him repeatedly.
But He never complained.
Thanks, Jesus, for enduring the pain.

MY HERO

Christ is my hero.
He saved the day.
And made a way.
For me to go to Heaven,
Christ will always be my hero.

HE WILL RETURN

Christ will come back.
This He has promised.
I will pray and wait.
For I know He will return.

CHRIST DIED ON THE CROSS.

Christ died on the cross.
He did it because we were lost
Thank you, Christ, for dying for me
Today, I can boldly say I am free
Put your trust in Him
He will forgive you for all your sin.

MY BLESSING

Christ is my blessing.
He came from Heaven.
To die for me.
He is my blessing.
Now I am free.

I AM READY

When Christ returns
I will not have to run.
He lives in my heart,
I am ready to go.
And be with Him.
What about you?

HE LEFT ME

I looked around for Christ,
Whom I could not see.
He left me.
Where did He go?
I know where He went.
He is in Heaven, waiting for me.

OBEY HIM

If you love Christ
because He died.
to save your life,
Then obey Him.
Open your heart,
and let Him in.

ON THE CROSS

Jesus died on the cross.
When I heard this, I thought I was lost.
He arose on the third day.
He came back to life just like He said.
But He did not come back to stay.
He is in Heaven with His Father.
Accept Him, for He is the only way.

INNOCENT BLOOD SHED

Jesus died on the cross
for a world that was lost.
He was in agony and pain as He bled.
All the innocent blood He shed.
To His heavenly Father, He cried.
Then He hung his head and died.

EASTER TIME

Today reminds me of that day.
When Christ died on the cross in such a cruel way.
But I believe in my heart that Christ is alive and in Heaven,
and He is seated next to God, His Father,
watching over me daily.

CHRIST IS IN HEAVEN

Christ lives in Heaven.
With God His Father.
He watches over me each day,
and I will always thank Him when I pray.

EASTER THANKS

Thank you, Jesus, for what you have done.
Thank you, Jesus, for carrying your cross alone.
Thank you, Jesus, for being nailed to the cross.
Thank you, Jesus, because of you, I am not lost.

LET HIS LIGHT SHINE

Before I met Jesus Christ,
Darkness filled my life.
Now that I know and love Him,
Let His light shine through me.

BEATEN

Christ, you were beaten,
but in your face, I saw humility.
I never saw any tears.
Christ, they beat you, and I saw no fear.
You knew this was the will of your Father.

WHY FOR ME?

Christ, I know I should not ask why.
To do what you have done tells it all.
You did not have to do it, why did you?
You saved me, and in my heart, you will always be.
Your love for me is real; this I hope you see.

CHRIST, PLEASE DON'T DIE

I stood near the cross in shock.
Standing there in disbelief,
I saw my Savior, bruised and weak.
I said to Him, "Christ, please don't die."
As I began to wipe the tears from my eyes,
It was at that moment He closed His eyes and died.

MY FRIEND

Where is Jesus Christ, my friend,
The one who stood by me until the end?
I want to give praise and thanks to Him,
The one who died for my sins.
Thank you, my precious friend.
I love you, and I will see you again.

THINGS I WILL DO FOR CHRIST

I will always love Him.
I will always pray to Him.
I will tell my friends about Him every day.
Because of what He has done for me, I cannot repay Him.
Christ, I love you for dying on the cross that day.

TODAY I FEEL BLESSED

A long, long time ago,
Christ died on the cross for me.
He came back to life so that I could be free.
Now He is in Heaven preparing a place for me.
Today I feel blessed, can't you see?

I HONOR YOU

Christ, you were humble.
Many times, I saw you fall.
But you always got up,
and continued up the hill.
Christ, you deserve honor,
and today, I honor you.

AN EMPTY TOMB

After the death of my Savior and Lord,
The soldiers placed Him in a borrowed tomb.
I watched as they laid Him down.
Only my heavenly Father could have known.
That in three days, an empty tomb would be found.
I walked to the tomb that day.
He was not there, so I ran away.
At that moment, I knew I had nothing to fear.
Because Christ died, and yet He lives,
and to all who believe in Him, eternal life He gives.

UP CALVARY'S HILL

Oh, how hard it must have been.
To carry a cross up Calvary's Hill back then.
Christ carried His cross and never complained.
He knew He had to do His Father's will.

Christ knew He would die on the cross,
and arose to save the lost.
How blessed are we when we accept Him.
When we do, we are no longer bound in sin.

HE CARRIED HIS CROSS

Christ was beaten, kicked, and tossed,
and made to carry His cross.
Through all His suffering and pain,
He proved to be a forgiving man.
Because He asked His Father to forgive all,
for they knew not what they were doing
Or even why He had to die on the cross.
Some laughed, and some cried,
As Christ hung His head and died.

TODAY CHRIST LIVES

One day our Savior was nailed to a cross.
He did it to save us because we were lost.
Our Savior was laughed at, mocked, and probed.
The soldiers had no shame; they gambled for His robe.
I can imagine our Savior was tired and thirsty.
They were cruel to Him and offered Him no water.
But Christ took all they did to Him.
He never said anything to the men.
On the ninth hour, Christ was dead.
I believe that He will be back like He said.
Christ resurrected, and today He lives.

BOUND IN CHAINS

I was born into a world full of sin.
I was bound in chains and refused to let Christ in.
I was holding on to things of the world, it seemed.
I felt dirty, unloved, and unclean.
Today my heart is filled with love.
Because I realized why Jesus died on the cross,
and I know His blood has made me pure.
Heaven is my eternal home, I am sure.

CHRIST, WAIT, I WILL GO WITH YOU.

My precious Lord and Savior,
Who came to die on the cross for me,
I saw how the people treated you,
You were kicked and beaten.
I cannot bear to see you go to the cross alone.
Christ, please wait; I will go with you.
He told me to wait and trust Him
And He would return for His faithful few

CHRIST, CAN YOU WALK WITH ME?

My burdens are heavy and unbearable sometimes.
People laugh and tell me I am out of my mind.
Because I believe Christ died on the cross for me.
They say I am odd for believing He did, and how could that be?
Sometimes I feel like I am all alone.
Why can't people believe what Christ has done?
Christ, my heart is heavy; can you walk with me?
He told me yes because He would die to set you free.

JESUS CHRIST

J is for the joy that only Christ can give.
E is for eternal life, He promised us.
S is for the suffering He endured for you and me.
U is for understanding; He knows what we go through.
S is for sinlessness; He was born without sin.

C is for crucifixion; He died in such a cruel way.
H is for the hope that He gives us each day.
R is for the risen one; He rose from the dead.
I is for intercessor; He talks to God for all who believe.
S is for sacrifice; He gave His life for the world.
T is for the throne where He sits and watches all.

CHRIST DIED FOR ME

One day I thought I was lost.
I had no peace, hope, or joy.
Then someone told me about an old rugged cross,
Where Christ died for me.

Now I can stand tall and be glad,
For I have joy and love, and I am not sad.
Thank you, God. You gave your only son.
Now that I believe in Christ Jesus, my life has just begun.

CHRIST LIVES IN MY HEART

Today I feel special because Christ died for me.
You see, he died violently in a sad, cruel way.
But I know He still lives and is coming back one day.
Until then, I will be obedient and continue to pray.
Yes, I feel special today because Christ lives in my heart.
He gave me the Holy Spirit; no, He will never depart.
Yes, I feel special because Jesus died on the cross.
Today, I want you to know that you will never be lost if you accept Him.

NAILED TO THE CROSS

Jesus was nailed to the cross.
He was kicked, pushed, and tossed.
Pilate found no faults in Him.
But they nailed Him to the cross anyway.

He was mocked, teased, laughed at, and frowned upon,
and on His head, they made Him wear a crown of thorns.
But to Christ, that was okay.
Because He knew He would rise on the third day.

Yes, they nailed Him to the cross.
And today, I stand before you with joy,
I am not lost,
Because Christ died on the cross for me.

RESURRECTION JOY

What a joy it is to be alive on this Resurrection Day,
To celebrate the death and resurrection of Christ
in such an honorable way.
What a joy it is to stand before all of you,
to give praise to Christ, who died for me too.

What a joy it is to hear all the poems and songs
and to feel the love everyone has in their heart.
For I know one day, when my life is over, and I will have to depart,
The joy is knowing that I will be with Christ, my Savior.

EASTER DAY

E is for everlasting life through Christ Jesus.
A is for all the things He has given us.
S is for Savior because He is truly my Savior.
T is for the times I think about Him over and over.
E is for excellence, for He is in every way.
R is for resurrection, for He rose on the third day.
D is for divine because He was holy and sacred.
A is for answered prayers from Christ, my precious Savior.
Y is for yielding and letting you guide me daily, Christ Jesus.
Thank you for this beautiful day.
Happy Resurrection Day to all!

EASTER SONGS

Today I am reminded of many songs.
A special one that comes to my mind is "The Old Rugged Cross."
For that is where Christ died so that we would not be lost.
It is there on that cross Christ paid the ultimate cost.

Oh, and I cannot forget they crucified my Lord.
Even though He was found innocent by a man name Pilate,
The crowd yelled, "Crucify Him!"
They took Him and beat Him all night long.
Then they led Him up Calvary's Hill to carry His cross alone.

But He arose! He rose!
Yes, He rose from the dead for me.
He ascended into Heaven, feeling no pain.
He left His Holy Spirit to comfort me.

HE GAVE HIS LIFE

Christ gave His life for you and me.
Now I know His love for me is real.
He knew His life He had to give,
for all who believe in Him would die, yet lives.
Who else would give their life for me, a sinner?
God had His only son die because He wants me to enter Heaven.
He loves me so much; He made a way for me to live forever.
But that can only happen if we trust Christ as our Savior.

IF CHRIST HAD NOT DIED

I was born into a world full of sin.
I had no desire in my heart to let Christ in.
In my mind, I did not need anything.
And oh, what happy songs I would sing.

But now I know if Christ had not died,
I would be lost, with nowhere to hide.
And because He died, today I am free.
I love Him because He did it for me.

If Christ had not died on Calvary's Cross,
We would all be confused, bound, and lost.
But because of our heavenly Father's mercy,
We all have eternal life if we believe,
that Christ was once dead, but now He lives.

FORGIVE ME, CHRIST

Christ, I have done many terrible things in my life.
I am ashamed of some things that were not so nice.
Christ, how can I come to you when you are perfect?
I am ashamed of what I have done, some I cannot correct.
But someone told me about you dying on the cross for me.
I said, "I didn't deserve it; why would He?"
Christ, it took a long time for me to understand.
Why you willingly went to the cross and die that day.
I know now that you did it to take my sins away.
Christ, I accept you today with all my heart.
Please forgive me for all the wrong I have done.
I realize now, Christ, that you are the Almighty one.

WHERE WOULD I BE?

If Christ had not died on the cross,
I would be in this sinful world lost.
There would be no happiness and no joy.
I would be an unhappy boy.

But since He died and arose on the third day,
I will always thank Christ in my special way.
I want to be more like Him every day.
I will not forget to thank Him every time I pray.

THEY CRUCIFIED MY SON

My name is Mary; I am the mother of Jesus.
I was there on that sad, sad day.
I watched them treat my son in such a cruel way.
They beat, kicked, and mocked Him; all I could do was pray.

They crucified my son on the cross
So the world would not be lost.
On that day, He wore a purple robe,
and they placed on His head a crown made of thorns.

They put Him on a cross between two thieves.
I watched in disbelief and fell to my knees,
because in my son, they found no fault.
He was able to conquer death, Hell,
and the grave so our souls would not be lost.

CHRIST RESURRECTED

I know Christ rose from the dead.
I talk to Him before I go to bed.
He lives in my heart.
He leads me and guides me day and night.
He makes sure that I always do what is right.

I know Christ rose on the third day,
Because His tomb was found empty, the Bible says.
No one knew what had happened or where He had gone.
His body was put in a tomb.

Christ had resurrected and was among His disciples.
They were in disbelief that it was Jesus.
Especially Thomas, to whom He showed His hands.
Christ had resurrected and went to be with them again.

I WILL HONOR AND
PRAISE YOU, CHRIST

Christ, I honor you because God gave you, His only son,
and because He did, you hung, bled, and died.
Christ, I honor you because through accepting your death and resurrection,
my new life has begun.
I honor you because you are the way, the truth, and the life.

Christ, I praise you because you saved my soul.
I praise You because, through You, the truth is told.
Christ, I praise you for teaching me to do what is right.
All praises and honors to you, Christ,
because through you, I can see the light.

HE IS COMING BACK

Some believe Christ never died.
on the cross,
Therefore, how could He
come back to life?

Some say He is not a Savior,
Many believe He is just another man,
to whom God showed favor.

But I stand before you today,
to tell you Christ did die on the cross,
and He resurrected on the third day.

If you do not believe He did,
Your soul is already lost.
Christ is coming back.
For all who believe in Him, and this is a fact.

MY THANKS TO CHRIST

Christ, I thank you for what you did.
You were nailed to and died on the cross.
You did what you said you would do.
You took my sins along with you.
Christ, I thank you because you did not have to die.
You obeyed your heavenly Father and did it anyway.
I thank you, Christ, for being my Lord and Savior.
Christ, I thank you for showing me unmerited favor.

A LETTER TO CHRIST

Dear Christ,

I want to thank you today for what you have done for me. I know you didn't have to do it, but you loved me so much that you suffered and died for me. I am sad about what the soldiers did to you. I know you gave your life for me, which is why I accept you in my heart and will always love you. Sometimes I think about how you died for me, and my love is not enough. I want to abide in you, and I want you to abide in me. I want to be more like you each day because you have given me a gift more precious than gold. Thanks to you, I have the gift of Salvation. Thank you for dying on the cross for me that day alone, long ago. One day I will see you in Heaven to thank you face to face; what a joyful day that will be.

Love,
Your name

THANKS TO GOD THE FATHER

Heavenly Father, I stand before you today.
To give all praises and thanks to you in a humble way.
For I know in my heart that you did not have to give your only son
to die when He did nothing wrong.

Heavenly Father, I thank you for loving me so dearly.
I know when you sat and watched from your throne,
You were pleased with what your son had done.
He made you proud, for He listened and obeyed.

Heavenly Father, my love for you will never die.
In Christ, your son, I will always abide.
I know He died so sad and cruel as He hung on the cross.
He resurrected and is seated on the throne next to you.
Thank you, God the Father.

WELCOME TO THE PROGRAM

Welcome, welcome, welcome, this beautiful Resurrection Day.
Welcome to the house of God, where we come to sing, worship, and pray.
Please get ready to enjoy yourselves with what we have to say.
We want to share this with you.
The reason Christ died on the cross.
Welcome, welcome, welcome, and Happy Resurrection Day!

A RESURRECTION DAY PROGRAM PRAYER

Heavenly Father, we want to give all honor and praise to you. Father, we thank you for this Resurrection Day, for it is the time of year when we can sit and think about our Lord and Savior and what He has done for us. Father, thank you for allowing your only begotten son to go to the cross and die for sinners like us. Father, we didn't deserve it, and we thank you. He not only went to the cross and died, but you raised Him from the dead so that we may have eternal life if we believe in Him. Father, we thank you for being such a loving God, for we know that you did not have to do it, but you did because you love us more than anything. We want to do what is pleasing to you.

Father, we ask that you bless this program and all the participants. And Father God, we pray that if there is anyone here who does not know you. We hope they will come to know you through this program. Father, we thank you and ask it all in Christ's name. Amen.

Christmas Program

BORN TO DIE

Jesus was born.
To die for me,
and now I am free.

HAIL TO THE KING

He will bring joy.
To every girl and boy.
Hail to the King.
A happy song I will sing.

CHRIST MAKES ME SMILE

I am a happy child,
Because Christ talks to me,
when I am sad, this is why,
Christ makes me smile.

THANKS TO GOD

Christ was born.
To be with me.
Thanks to you, God,
I am never alone.

WHO IS THIS BABY?

I heard about a baby.
Born to a special lady,
He was born free of sin.
Who is this baby?
The one who was born in a place,
not fit for a king.
He is Jesus Christ our Savior.

GOD'S ONLY SON

A baby was born,
God's only son.
A baby was born.
To bear the cross all alone.

I WILL

I will give you thanks.
I will give you praise.
I will give you honor.
Just because you were born,
to one day die for me.
Thank you, Jesus Christ.

HE BROUGHT JOY

A baby boy,
One who brought joy,
into my little heart.
Thank you, Father God,
because you are smart.

BABY JESUS

Baby Jesus was born free of sin.
Open your heart and let Him in.
Baby Jesus was born to be loved.
He is a gift from Heaven above.

LOTS OF LOVE

A sweet baby boy,
He had so much joy,
and lots of love,
to share with all.
From His Father who is in Heaven.

HOLY AND DIVINE

A precious baby born to be mine,
One who was born holy and divine.
Christ was perfect in every way.
I live my life to be more like Him each day.

CHRIST'S BIRTH MAKES ME HAPPY

When I heard of His birth,
I was the happiest girl on Earth.
Thank you, Jesus.
Your birth made me happy.

MY BLESSING

Christ is my blessing.
He came from Heaven.
To die for me.
He is my blessing.
Can't you see?
I am willing to share,
Because His Salvation is free.

I AM READY

When Christ returns
I will not have to run.
He lives in my heart.
I am ready to leave.
And go with Him.
What about you?

HE LEFT ME

I looked around.
For Christ, whom
I could not see.
He left me; where did He go?
He is in Heaven,
waiting for you and me.

CHRISTMAS, A TIME TO SHARE

Christmastime is here.
Christmas is a time to share,
A time to show all you care.
God cared; He gave us His only son.
God shared His love with everyone.

WELCOME

Welcome, welcome, welcome.
Sit back, enjoy, and be blessed.
As we tell you, the real reason.
For this happy holiday season.

WHO IS THIS BABY JESUS?

He is God's only begotten son,
Born to bear our sins alone.
He is our precious Lord and Savior,
The one who came to show us favor.

I LOVE YOU, CHRIST

You were born for me,
and you came to set me free.
I love you, Christ.
Because you have changed my life.
Thank you for being born,
God's only begotten, son.

ONE WHO WAS BLESSED

Christ was blessed.
By God, His Father
From the time He was born,
for He was God's only son.
Christ never had to fear.
His father was always nearby.

A SILENT NIGHT

As the day turned into darkness
And the stars shone bright,
It was a holy and silent night.
That was when our Savior was born.
He was born for all to see the light.

A TIME FOR GIVING

Christmas is a time for giving,
and a time for believing.
In the only divine being,
The one whom God gave to save us all.
Please accept this gift of Salvation; it is free.
He is the only answer for the world today.
Invite Him into your heart, and He will never go away.

A HOLY NIGHT

It was a holy night.
The stars shined bright.
Everything seemed so right.
A precious baby was born.
What a beautiful sight.
As He slept in His manger quietly,
Mary and Joseph looked on proudly.
For they knew with all their heart,
A King was born on that holy night.

BORN TO SAVE ALL

A baby born holy and divine,
One whom I can surely call mine,
He came to give me peace.
He came to give me joy.
This precious baby boy
Was born to save all.
Please come to Him when you hear His call.

MERRY CHRISTMAS

Merry Christmas to everyone.
To us, a baby was born, so tiny and small.
He will bring us peace and joy.
God has blessed the world.
With His holy gift, a baby boy.
Merry Christmas, and God bless all.

A KING WAS BORN

One night many years ago,
A baby was born with a special glow.
Only our heavenly Father could have known,
On that night, a King would be born.

This King was born without sin.
Please open your heart and let Him in.
Why live your life in darkness,
When King Jesus was born to give you light.

THE GREATEST GIFT

I was given a special gift from Mom.
Dad gave me all the things I asked for.
My grandma and grandpa gave me lots of love.
But the greatest gift came from Heaven above.
That gift was my precious Lord and Savior.
Accept Him today, and God will grant you favor.

BORN WITHOUT SIN

Christ was born without sin.
He is the only one who can take sin away.
We must open our hearts and let Him in.
Christ loves us and He proved it one day.
He went to the cross and died humbly.
He did not have to do it, but He did because He loves us.
If He had not died, our lives would be a mess.
Christ, we love you, and you are the best.

CHRIST, YOU CAN HAVE MY BED

I heard about a baby who was born with no bed.
He had nowhere to sleep and no place to lay His little head.
I was always taught to share.
Christ, because of your birth, I care.
It's okay; you can have my bed.
God will bless me with another one to lay my head.

HATED BY MANY; LOVED BY FEW

Jesus, who was born King of the Jews,
He knew He was hated by many and loved by few.
People talked about and mocked Him; this He knew.
Christ showed His love for everyone.
He went to the cross and died, God's only son.

HATED BY THE KING

When the King heard of His birth,
He wanted to search all parts of the Earth.
He wanted baby Jesus found and brought to him.
But God knew the King's heart.
He knew the King hated Christ.
God sent angels who told Joseph to depart.
They left the town of David for a new start.

A HOLY BABY

I came to worship this holy baby,
One who was born in a stable,
Worthy of worship and praises,
A blessed baby born our Lord and Savior.
Thank you, God, because you saw a need.
To send your son into a world so full of sin,
To be our Lord and Savior and to be our friend.

LET US WORSHIP THIS BABY.

Some will hate this baby.
Some will love this baby.
Some will want to kill this baby.
But I say to everyone,
Let us all worship this baby.

THE GREATEST GIFT

I received gifts.
Some of them I kept.
Some made me laugh,
And some made me cry.
But the greatest gift of all.
Is the one God is giving us out of love.
Jesus is this gift sent from Heaven above.

AN AMAZING BIRTH

God showed favor to a woman one day.
He knew His son's birth was the only way.
To save His people from the sin they were born in.
Christ was conceived miraculously through the Holy Spirit.
This is why His birth is so amazing.

THE PROMISE SAVIOR HAS COME

The promise has come to all,
He was born to pay a debt that we owe,
No matter whether we are rich or poor,
A debt owes, but we will owe no more when He dies.
Jesus was born to pay the price.
The debt will be paid with His life.
He has come so we can live.
Born to die, His life He was willing to give.

BOUND BY SIN

Before Christ, our Savior was born,
I was lost in sin.
I did not know which way to go,
But now that Christ, my Savior, is here,
I can go anywhere without fear.
Christ, since I opened my heart and let you in,
I am not bound by sin.

THANK YOU FOR COMING

You have heard poems read from our hearts.
You have heard how Christ can give you a new start.
You have seen the joy we have in knowing Christ.
You have heard the children singing.
Now we want to thank you for coming.
Thank you, and God bless you.

CHRISTMASTIME

Christmas is a time to give all thanks and praises,
to Christ, who was born to be our Savior.
Mary, whom God showed great favor,
was blessed when God chose her to carry our Savior.
A time to reflect on God's precious gift.
And a time to give thanks to Him for His kindness.
One can give me gold or silver,
But no one can out-give God, the greatest giver.

MIRACLE BABY

The baby everyone traveled from afar to see,
The one who would die to set the world free.
Who is this miracle baby?
He is Christ our Lord and Savior.

LET US WORSHIP THIS BABY.

He who was born into this world,
The one who should be praised and loved,
Let every man, woman, boy, and girl,
Worship this holy baby,
The one who was born of a virgin lady.

God knew He wanted Mary to carry,
and give birth to His only son.
Let us worship and share the news.
For this baby would be crowned King of the Jews,
and one day suffer and die to save the world.
Let us worship this baby boy.
He came to bring eternal life and joy.

NO PLACE TO CALL HOME

Our Lord and Savior was born in a stable,
Given birth by a woman who was shown favor.
He had no place to lay His head.
His parents found a manger and made it His bed.
There He lay peacefully upon the hay.
His mother closely watched as He lay.
He had no place to call His home.
But God, His Father in Heaven, never left Him alone.
He was proud of His only son.
Who would one day die to save His people.
And afterward, return to His heavenly home,
Seated next to His Father on the throne.

A BABY, A SAVIOR

What an honor it must have been
To be born a holy baby for all to see,
A unique baby for the world to love,
A beautiful baby sent from Heaven above,
A baby born to be worshiped by all,
A Savior who was born to save the world,
A Savior who knew He would die on the cross,
A Savior who conquered death, Hell, and the grave,
A Savior who returned with the keys in His hands,
A Savior who knew His Father's divine plan,
whose desire is to give eternal life to everyone.

CHRISTMAS MEMORIES

A baby born on a chilly night,
A baby born in a stable, lying in a manger,
A baby who brought joy to the shepherds,
A baby born to be King of Kings and Lord of Lords,
A baby born to be King of the Jews,
A baby who brought the world good news,
A baby who was born the son of the Living God.
A baby who is called Wonderful Counselor,
A baby who would bring peace to us on Earth,
A baby who was born of a virgin birth,
A baby born of a woman to whom God showed favor,
This baby is now Christ, our Lord and Savior.

A GIFT FROM HEAVEN

I have received gifts from my father and mother.
My siblings also gave me gifts,
but what a blessing to receive a gift from Heaven,
A gift I will always treasure.
My heavenly Father took such pleasure.
He gave us a gift so undeserving.
For all to unwrap and receive,
A gift that will bring Salvation if you believe.
If you accept this gift, it cannot be returned.
But if you do not, in the fire, you will burn.
This gift from Heaven will bring you peace.
Please accept Jesus, for He is yours to keep.

JESUS LOVES THE LOST

He was born to set me free,
from all the sins I carried within.
Jesus loves me, I can plainly see.
One day He will die on a cross,
to show how much He loves the lost.
A little baby was born to be a comforter.
God must really care for us.
He made a way for us to enter.
His glorious and beautiful kingdom.
Yes, Jesus loves us,
and I know the day will come.
When He will say to all, who accept Him.
He will say well done to all His faithful servants.

BORN IN A STABLE

The Savior of this world
Was born in a stable.
There in a manger, He lay,
so wonderfully made.

The night was silent and cold.
He was wrapped in swaddling clothes.
As He lay gently upon a pile of hay,
Born to save the world one day.

Yes, He was born in a stable.
There He laid, so gentle and small.
God, His Father, was with Him through it all,
and today, Christ is with us forever.

BORN TO DIE FOR YOU AND ME

An innocent newborn baby,
So precious to His mother, Mary,
was born to die for you and me.
And to set the world free.

All will worship this baby.
King of all Kings, He will be called.
Everyone rejoiced when they heard the news.
This newborn baby would be King of the Jews.

What peace you should have,
Knowing the reason for His birth.
He was born here on Earth
to suffer and die for the world.

UNDERNEATH THE STARS

There lay a baby boy,
One who would be named Jesus.
He would bring the world joy.
In a tiny manger, He lay,
Beautifully and wonderfully made.
Underneath the stars that night,
A Savior was born to show us light,
And He will guide us to do what is right.

FOLLOW THAT STAR.

From the east, I saw a star.
It was shining brighter than the others.
I gathered all I had together.
I left to follow that star.
I traveled nights and days,
Not letting anything get in my way.
I had to understand why.
That one star was different from the others.
I got there and stood underneath the unique star.
I saw it was shining upon a special baby boy.
At that moment, my heart was full of joy.
I was glad I followed that star,
which was very far.

THANK YOU, GOD

Thank you, God, for the divine plan you have.
Thank you for the one and only son you gave.
Thank you for His birth on that holy night.
Thank you because He came to give the world light.

Thank you for being so kind and merciful.
Thank you, God; I know it must be painful.
To send your son to be born in a world so sinful.
Thank you, God, because you knew what He would go through.

And when all is done, He will only be loved by a few.
Thank you, God; you loved me enough to send.
Your only son to be my Savior and friend.
Thank you, God, for when my life is over, I will see you in the end.

WELCOME

Welcome to the house of the Lord.
We have poems, songs, and more.
Sit back, open your heart, and enjoy.
Before you leave, you will understand,
what was so special about this baby boy.
Welcome, everyone.

A CHRISTMAS PRAYER

Father God, first, we want to give all honor and praise to you. We thank you for your kindness and your mercy. Father, we thank you for sending your only son to be born into a world that is hateful, mean, and full of sin. Father, we know you did not have to allow Him to be born in a world to be hated by so many, but you did, and we thank you. We thank you for Jesus Christ, who was born to save us. Father God, we thank you for this gift you have given us, a precious gift of love. We do not deserve it, but we thank you for Him.

Now, Father God, we ask that you bless this program and all the participants. We pray that it will touch someone and that he or she will ask, "What must I do to be saved?" In Christ's name we pray. Amen.

Christmas and Resurrection Day Skits

A WALK TO THE CRUCIFIXION

Cast: Two kids, ages ten through twelve

Person 1—I was there that morning when it all started.

Person 2—You mean when Christ was brought before the governor?

Person 1—I was among the crowd yelling, "Crucify Him!" But I remained silent. The governor found no fault in Christ, but the people wanted Him dead, and they all yelled, "Crucify Him!"

Person 2—I thought there were two men, and the crowd had to choose one who would live.

Person 1—They chose Christ to die and the sinner to go free.

Person 2—So they are going to kill an innocent man?

Person 1—Yes, and I want to be near Him and show Him I am here if He needs me. Now, I will follow Him up Calvary's hill.

Person 2—Christ will not know you are in the crowd.

Person 1—You are right, but it is okay.

Person 2—Come on, I will walk with you.

Person 1—Christ is a good man. He loves everybody, and He has done so much for us.

Person 2—It is such a shame they want to kill Him. He has done nothing wrong, yet He is going willingly.

Person 1—Someone told me He is doing this because it is the will of His Father.

Person 2—But how can a father let His son be nailed to a cross and die horribly and not try to help him?

Person 1—For us!

Person 2—What do you mean?

Person 1—Right now, we are sinners and lost in sin. God loves us and does not want death to be our final destiny. Therefore, He sent His only son to die for all our sins.

Person 2—Oh wow! What a merciful and loving God to allow His one and only son to die for a sinner like me.

Person 1—I also heard that Christ will not stay dead. He will rise in three days.

Person 2—Wait a minute! I feel scared. I thought once you die, you will be gone forever.

Person 1—That is true, but there is something different about Christ. He has the power to do all things.

Person 2—What do you mean? What things can He do?

Person 1—I have heard about some of His miracles. He raised people who were dead, healed the sick, and fed the homeless.

Person 2—So will He raise Himself from the dead?

Person 1—No, but His heavenly Father will. He has all power in His hands.

Person 2—What will happen when Christ comes back to life? What will He do? Where will He go?

Person 1—He will be among His people for a few days to comfort them. Then He will ascend to Heaven to be seated on the throne with His Father. But He will leave His Holy Spirit to live in all believers.

Person 2—When you say "believers," whom exactly are you talking about?

Person 1—Believers believe with all their hearts that Jesus is God's son and was raised from the dead. They will admit that they are sinners and put their faith in Christ. They should ask for forgiveness and invite the Holy Spirit to live in them.

Person 2—If they believe and do these things, they will be saved and have eternal life through Christ.

Person 1—Yes!

Person 2—Let me make sure I understand. God loves us, and because of His love and mercy, He is giving us a gift of Salvation through His son Jesus, and all who accept the gift of Salvation will have everlasting life.

Person 1—Yes, it is just that simple. As easy as saying, "One, two, three."

Person 2—Can you tell me about Heaven, Hell, and the Lake of Fire?

Person 1—Those places are all real, though some people may tell you they are not. Heaven is where all believers' souls will rest when they die. Because the Bible says to be absent from the body is to be present with the Lord, this is meant for Christians. Heaven is a beautiful place of lightness, happiness, and joy. Hell is where non-believers' souls will be tormented until Judgment Day. It is a place of darkness and sadness. Once you are there, all hope is lost. The Lake of Fire is real. All who have rejected Christ will go there once they have been judged. They will be thrown into the Lake of Fire with Satan, and they will all die a second death spiritually and be separated from God forever.

Person 2—Wow! What an earful. Who in their right mind would want to go there when all they must do is accept God's gift of Salvation?

Person 1—It is sad, but many people have and will continue to reject Christ because of their selfish pride and lust for the things of the world.

Person 2—Before talking to you, I did not know what all this meant or why Christ had to die, but now I understand. I understand the plan of Salvation. I must accept Christ as my Savior to see Him again.

Person 1—That is right! You know, while we were talking, the crucifixion took place. Christ has died.

Person 2—I am not sad anymore because I know He is coming back for me one day because I am a true believer.

Person 1—I am glad Christ is no longer suffering; I know He will resurrect in a few days. I am not sad anymore, either. We will both see Him again.

Both—Christ, we love you and have accepted your death and resurrection. (To the audience) Have you?

I MUST DIE

Cast: Christ and a child aged four through six

Girl—Christ, I heard about you when you were born.

Christ—What did you hear, my child?

Girl—I heard you were born in a manger, and you were born to die for me.

Christ—Yes, I came so you can have everlasting life.

Girl—Christ, what is everlasting life, and why will you die to give it to me?

Christ—Everlasting life is life after death, and I must die so you and all the people who accept me can live forever.

Girl—But Christ, I am alive. We are all living.

Christ—My precious child, I know you are alive, and I am alive too. But before you can have everlasting life, I must die.

Girl—Who told you that you must die?

Christ—My Father in Heaven said that I must die for you.

Girl—You mean you will die for me?

Christ—Yes, my little one, and for all the rest of the world.

Girl—Is God okay with you dying?

Christ—Yes, it is His divine will for my life while I am here.

Girl—How will you die?

Christ—I will die on the cross.

Girl—Can you tell me again why you are doing this?

Christ—I am doing this to take your and all other people's sins to the cross with me, so you will no longer have to live in them.

Girl—My sins? What do you mean?

Christ—Well, do you always listen to your parents? Do you tell the truth all the time?

Girl—No, I do not.

Christ—Those are sins for which I must die.

Girl—Christ, you are nice.

Christ—There is something else I must tell you. When I die, I will not stay dead. I will come back to life.

Girl—Wow! How can you do that?

Christ—I cannot, but my Father can. He has the power to do all things.

Girl—Where is your father?

Christ—My Father lives in Heaven and watches over us daily.

Girl—You mean he can see me when I do terrible things?

Christ—Yes, He can, for He sees all things.

Girl—Is He my father too?

Christ—He is your Heavenly Father also.

Girl—When you take my sins away after you die on the cross, will I sin again?

Christ—Yes, you will, for you are not perfect. But because I will go to the cross and die for your sins, you have the right to ask me for forgiveness if you believe in me. I will then talk it over with my Father, and He will forgive you if you meant it from your heart.

Girl—What happens if I continue to sin?

Christ—My Father will be unhappy with you and must punish you, but if you believe in me, your goal should be to try not to sin.

Girl—I love you, Christ, and I do not want to make God mad. I will always try to do what is right.

Christ—This will be pleasing to my Father.

Girl—Christ, where will you go when you return to life?

Christ—I will go back to Heaven to be with my Father. I will sit on the throne with Him, watching the good and the bad.

Girl—Can I go with you?

Christ—No, my child, not now. But one day, you will because I will prepare a place for all who believe in me.

Girl—When I need to talk to you, can I?

Christ—You can always talk to me, my precious child. When I leave here, I will leave my Holy Spirit to live in you and comfort you.

Girl—So I will not be alone?

Christ—No, my little one. I will always be in your heart, loving you and guiding you to do what is right. May joy and peace be with you until I see you again.

Girl—Goodbye, Christ; I love you and will tell all the people I know and meet about you and the good news you have shared with me.

Christ---Bless you; this is what all who believe in me should do. I love you, my innocent child.

WE CAN SAVE CHRIST;
I KNOW WE CAN

Setting: (The day before the crucifixion

Cast: Four children *aged nine to twelve* **and someone to be the voice of an adult)**

Person 1—Have you all heard the news about our Lord and Savior?

Person 2—No, what news?

Person 3—I heard something about a crucifixion.

Person 4—Yeah. They are going to kill our Lord and Savior.

Person 1—That is the news; we must save Him.

Person 2—Why will they kill Him? What has He done?

Person 3—Christ is innocent. He did not do anything wrong. He has never hurt anybody. He is a good man.

Person 4—I do not understand if He is a good man and has done nothing wrong, why should He die?

Person 1—I do not know, but He must.

Person 2—I am so confused; Christ has done nothing but good things. Why should He die?

Person 3—Yeah, He healed the sick, made the blind see and the lame walk.

Person 4—If He has done all these good things, why should He die?

Person 1—Guys, we can't let Him die. We must save Him. I know we can.

Person 2—How? We don't know where He is or what He is doing.

Person 3—Wherever He is, He is scared and sad. We must find Him and save Him; I know we can.

Person 4—Where will we go to look for Him?

Person 1—I know He is somewhere in the town of Jerusalem. He is not alone because twelve men follow Him. I hope they will protect Him until we can find Him.

Person 2—We must hurry because we don't have much time. We must get to Him before the Roman soldiers do.

Person 3—Before we leave, let us pray to our heavenly Father and ask Him to lead us to Christ. Surely, He would want to save His son.

Person 4—Yes, let us pray. Father God, please lead and guide us to our Lord and Savior. If we don't get to Him, He will be crucified, and we don't understand why. Can you help us find Him? He is your son, and I know you want to save Him. Will you help us? Amen.

Person 5—My precious children, yes, Christ is innocent, and I know He has done nothing wrong. But He is doing the will if His Father, and that is to die on the cross to save a lost world.

Person 1—But how will His death save the world?

Person 5—Right now, all people are lost in sin, and Christ is the only hope for everyone. His Father sent Him down from Heaven to save the world. He must die on the cross. I loves us so much and He is willing to let His son die so we can be forgiven for our sins and have eternal life through Christ, His son.

Person 2—So Christ must die, and we can't save Him?

Person—Yes, He must die, for this is His Father's will.. But He will resurrect on the third day and ascend to Heaven to be with His Father. He will be seated at my right hand forever, interceding for all who believe in Him.

Person 3—So Christ is going to die, but He will come back to life, and we can still talk to Him, and He will always be our Savior?

Person 5—Yes, Christ will always be our Savior. When He leaves us, He will leave His Holy Spirit to abide in all who accept Him, and He will always be the light of the world.

Person 1—Well, guys, we don't have to save Him. God has spoken to us, and now we know that Christ must die for us. It is God's will.

Person 2—I am so happy that Christ loves me so much that He will die for me. I sure do not feel like I deserve it.

Person 3—We don't have to save Him; God will save Him by bringing Him back to life. Wow! This news is so excellent. I want to scream thank you, Jesus.

Person 4—God is the best. He is willing to give His one and only son to die for us on the cross so that if we believe in Him, we will have eternal life. This is excellent news.

Person 1—I believe!

Person 2—I believe!

Person 3—I believe!

Person 4—I believe!

All— (turns to the congregation and says, "Do you?" Happy Resurrection Day!

WE MUST TELL THE GOOD NEWS

Setting: The Night Christ Was Born

Cast: one girl, two boys

Girl—This night is so quiet and beautiful; it feels different.

Boy 1—I know, even the stars shine brighter than usual.

Girl—There is a stillness about this night.

Boy 1—What do you think is going on?

Girl—I do not have a clue.

Boy 2—Haven't you all heard the good news about the baby?

Girl—What baby?

Boy 1—What news can be so good that it could make this night so different?

Boy 2—In the city of David, in an old stable, a Savior has been born, and He is asleep in a manger.

Girl—What do you mean, a Savior has been born?

Boy 1—Whom was He born to save, and from what?

Boy 2—He was born to save the world from the penalty of their sin.

Girl—Sin? I have never heard that word.

Boy 1—I have not, either. Can you tell us what sin is?

Boy 2—Sin is doing something that God says not to do.

Girl—Oh, you mean when you do not listen to your parents.

Boy 1—Or, if you steal something?

Boy 2—God is not happy when we do such things.

Girl— *(laughing aloud)* How can a baby save the world?

Boy 1—Yeah! That sounds sad. A baby who can save the world that's not right!

Boy 2—If you want to see for yourselves, follow me to the stable. When you see Him, then you will believe me.

Girl— *(looking through a peephole)* Hey! I see the special baby and His mother and I want to bow down and worship Him!

Boy 1— *(looking through another peephole)* I do not believe it! There is a baby lying in a manger, and there is something special about Him. I will bow down and worship Him too!

Boy 2—I also bowed down and worshiped Him when I saw Him. He was worthy of my worship.

Girl—The moment I saw the baby with His mother, my heart changed.

Boy 1—You know, I did not believe you, but this baby has changed my heart too.

Boy 2—Now that we have seen this baby and worshiped Him, we must go out and tell everyone the good news.

Girl—What will we say about Him?

Boy 1—And how should we say it?

Boy 2— (to the girl) When you saw the baby, you bowed down and worshiped Him.

Boy 2— (to the boy) And you bowed too. You both had a feeling of joy that only Christ could have given you.

Girl and Boy 1—But what does all this mean?

Boy 2—It means that only Christ can change your heart.

Girl—Yes, but what is the good news?

Boy 2—This tiny baby brings eternal life to all who believe in Him. He is a gift from God our Father, who loves us so much He is willing to give us a way to be forgiven of our sins through Christ, this baby who will die for us one day.

Girl—That is fantastic news!

Boy 1—Are you saying this baby will die for the entire world one day?

Boy 2—Yes, and on the third day, He will resurrect, ascend into Heaven, and wait for all believers who die in Him.

Boy 1—If we believe these things, will we have eternal life?

Boy 2—Yes! That is the good news that we must go and tell.

Girl—Wow! I had never had anyone die for me before. I will tell all the girls about this baby who will be our Savior because He was born to die for us.

Boy 1—I will go and tell all the boys.

Boy 2—And I will tell the rest of the people about this Savior who was born to save the people of this world if they will only believe.

All—Let us all go and tell the good news; He has come to save us. Merry Christmas to all!

A FREE GIFT

Cast: Two children, age six, having a conversation about when Christ was born

Child 1—Hey! I was given a free gift for Christmas.

Child 2—No way! Nobody gets a free gift; our parents must buy them.

Child 1—Not the gift about which I am talking. This one is free.

Child 2—Can you tell me where my parents can get this gift? Sometimes when I ask for things, they say, "We don't have any money." Surely, they wouldn't complain about a free gift.

Child 1—I will gladly tell you how to receive this free gift.

Child 2—Where can I go to get it? What store is it in?

Child 1—This gift is not in a store.

Child 2—Then how can I get it?

Child 1—The free gift I got for Christmas was baby Jesus, who was born, and I believe with all my heart that He is the son of God.

Child 2—A baby? What makes Him a gift?

Child 1—He was born to give the gift of Salvation.

Child 2—Salvation? I have no idea what you are talking about.

Child 1—Have you heard of Heaven?

Child 2—Yes, I have heard my parents talk about Heaven a few times.

Child 1—Do you want to go to Heaven when you die?

Child 2—Not if I have to die to get there.

Child 1—Well, we all must die one day, and we make the choice where we want to spend eternal life while we are living.

Child 2—Yes, I would choose Heaven. I have heard that my grandmother is there, and I would love to see her again.

Child 1—Well, before you can get there, you must accept this gift Christ came to give you.

Child 2—How do I accept this gift?

Child 1—Believe in your heart that Jesus is God's son and that He was born to die on the cross for your sins, and God His raised Him from the dead.

Child 2—Hey, wait a minute! You never talked about Christ being dead and coming back to life.

Child 1—Christ was born to die for our sins, and He will come back to life.

Child 2—So, if I believe I will receive this gift?

Child 1—Yes, the gift of Salvation

Child 2—Wow! This is so easy.

Child 1—Do you believe with all your heart?

Child 2—Yes, I do.

Child 1—Now that you have accepted the gift Christ was born to give, you are on your way to Heaven.

Child 2—Will I see my grandmother again?

Child 1—Yes, you will.

Child 2—Can I give this gift to my mom and dad?

Child 1—No, but Christ can. All you must do is tell them why Christ was born and that He will one day die for them. It is up to them to accept Christ's Salvation as their gift from God.

Child 2—I will tell them because I want to see them in Heaven.

Child 1—This is the best news you can share with anybody. Go out and tell your friends! They may not know about Jesus. May God bless you, and have a Merry Christmas!

COME AND LET US
WORSHIP THE BABY.

Cast: Three children, ages ten through twelve

Person 1—There was a baby born last night.

Person 2—So what? Babies are born every day. Why are you announcing this one?

Person 3—Yeah! Give me a break. I see babies all the time.

Person 1—But this baby was born to be a king and a great ruler.

Person 2—What your are saying doeesn't make since.

Person 3—We already have kings and great rulers. We don't need another one.

Person 1—But this one was born to rule throughout eternity. He will reign forever.

Person 2—Why are you all excited? We won't be around forever.

Person 3—Yeah! We will be long gone by then.

Person 1—True, but we are around today, and we should go and worship the baby.

Person 2—Now you are talking silly.

Person 3—I am not going to worship a baby!

Person 1—Well, let me tell you why and how this baby came into this world

Person 2—(yawning) Boring!

Person 3—Do we have to hear this?

Person 1—No! But if you do, it will bless both of you.

Person 2—Can we at least sit down?

Person 3—Is this going to be a long story?

Person 1—Once you hear the story of baby Jesus, you will understand. *(Persons 2 and 3 sit.)*

Person 1—There once was a woman whom God showed favor to bear His only son because God knew the world needed a Savior.

Person 2—I do not need a Savior.

Person 3—Me, either. I can save myself. I am strong. Look! See my muscles?

Person 1—Guys, Can I finish telling the story, please?

Person 2—Sure!

Person 3— Go ahead!

Person 1—The woman God found favor in was a virgin, but she would give birth to a baby. She was the chosen one.

Person 3—I bet she felt special to be chosen by God.

Person 1—I am sure she felt honored to give birth to this miracle baby.

Person 3—What makes this baby such a miracle?

Person 1—This baby came straight from God. He was conceived through the Holy Spirit. The power of God came upon His mother, Mary, and she conceived. The baby would be born holy and called the son of the living God.

Person 2—What do you mean, He was born holy?

Person 1—He was born without sin because He was born through the Holy Spirit.

Person 3—Are we holy?

Person 1—No, we were born in sin.

Person 2—Why?

Person 1—Because we are descendants of Adam and Eve. They committed the first sin when they ate from the Tree of Knowledge. That is how sin entered the world. Adam and Eve were the first man and woman; we were born through their bloodline. Therefore, we were born into sin. They had two boys, Cain and Abel. Cain committed the second sin when he killed his brother.

Person 2—Wow! This news is getting interesting!

Person 3—So, because we were born in sin, the only one who can free us is Christ the one who was born without sin?

Person 1—I understand it now; this is why baby Jesus was unique; because He is the son of God, and He was born without sin.

Person 3— This baby was born for us because we were born in sin, and today we are lost.

Person 2—I do not understand how God could send His son to a world so cruel and mean.

Person 1—He loves us and wants us to accept and trust His only son.

Person 2—Can I be holy like Christ?

Person 3—Me too! After hearing all of this, I want to be like Jesus.

Person 1—You can accept Christ and try to become more like Him each day. But because of sin, we will never be exactly like Him. God's grace will save us once we accept Christ's death and resurrection.

Person 2—What do you mean, Christ's death? Is Jesus going to die?

Person 1—Yes, He will die for us one day, but He will come back alive. If we believe with all our hearts that we are sinners and that Christ can save us because He is the son of God, then we are saved by God's grace.

Person 3—What is grace?

Person 1—Grace is the unmerited favor of God. We don't deserve it, but God loves us, so He gave it to us.

Person 2—You mean we don't have to work to receive grace?

Person 1—That is right! It is a gift from God.

Person 2—I feel bad for what I said about this baby. God, please forgive me.

Person 3—Please forgive me too.

Person 1—He will if you mean it with all your heart.

Person 2—I do and want to accept Him into my heart.

Person 3—I do too.

All—Now, we will go and worship this baby. He has come to save all of us. (Turn to the congregation and say together, "Happy Resurrection Day!")

A CHRISTMAS SKIT, JESUS IS THE REASON FOR THE SEASON!

(With some humor, have fun; the characters needed are two middle school girls.)

Girl 1---I love Christmas time.

Girl 2—Me too; I get to make this lengthy list of everything I want for Christmas.

Girl 1—I do not understand! Things?

Girl 2—Yes, things! I also want the new iPhone, iPad, computer, Bike, and that new game system.

Girl 1—Wow! Is this what Christmas means to you?

Girl 2—Why yes! This is what my parents taught me. What does it mean to you?

Girl 1—Christmas is about celebrating the birth of our Lord and Savior.

Girl 2—Our who and who?

Girl 1—Jesus Christ, the one who was born to die for our sins.

Girl 2—That doesn't sound true because who would die for others?

Girl 1—Jesus did! Do you and your family go to church?

Girl 2—I am happy to say yes! We go two times a year.

Girl 1—Wow! Just two times! That is sad. Why two times?

Girl 2—We get gifts for Christmas and Easter and have egg hunts and fun stuff. Also, the Easter bunny comes.

Girl 1—You do not know about Jesus; what church do you attend?

Girl 2—I go to Anything Goes Baptist Church.

Girl 1—Really? That is an odd name for a church.

Girl 2—Well, my mom and dad like it.

Girl 1—Okay! Whatever makes you all happy. Do you all go to Sunday School?

Girl 2—Sunday, who?

Girl 1—Sunday school!

Girl 2—No! I go to It is All Good Middle School.

Girl 1—Wow, another weird name; Sunday school is a part of church service where we learn about Jesus and how to live for Him.

Girl 2—Why do I need to know about Jesus? Can He give me gifts?

Girl 1—Oh yes, He can! He can give you the gift of Salvation.

Girl 2—Good, I like free stuff. Can you tell me more?

Girl 1—I will be happy to tell you more. God gave the ultimate gift. He sent His son to be born in a cruel world to die for us.

Girl 2—So God is nice?

Girl 1—Yes, He is! This is why we celebrate Christmas. It is all about Jesus Christ.

Girl 2—And Jesus was okay with being born to die?

Girl 1—Yes, because He and His Father love us that much. There is more good news.

Girl 2—More news! Wow! What is it?

Girl 1—Jesus did not stay dead; He arose and is now in Heaven.

Girl 2—And you learned all of this at your church in Sunday school?

Girl 1—Yes! And lots of other stuff.

Girl 2—I want this gift. How do I get it?

Girl 1—When you come to my house again, I will have my parents talk to you.

Girl 2—Okay, and once I accept this gift, I will tell my parents; they might want it too.

Girl 1—Hey, I just had a great thought; my parents can invite your parents to our church, and we can learn about Jesus together.

Girl 2—Yes! Awesome! Okay, talk to you later.

Now both girls will turn to the congregation and loudly say, "JESUS IS THE REASON FOR THE SEASON!"

More Poems and Speeches

WATCHED FROM ABOVE

Christ, our Savior, was born in the city of David.
From the time the King heard the news, Christ was hated.
An innocent baby loved by many and perfectly made,
God watched over Him in His manger as He lay.
He knew He would protect Him from harm's way.
This is why He led His parents and Him to Bethlehem to stay.
He loved His son and watched Him night and day.
From His throne, He sat and looked down with joy.
And He smiled at His wonderful baby boy.
He knew the price His son would pay one day.
God knew that His son would die on the cross.
He loved us and would save all who believed in His son.

JESUS IS ALL YOU NEED FOR CHRISTMAS

Christmas is a time when we enjoy giving.
It is also a time some just like receiving.
It is a time of year when kids are at their best.
They are asking parents for this and for that.
And parents are telling kids, "Just let me rest."
Mommies are asking daddies for diamonds and gold.
And daddies are saying, whatever you want is good."
Throughout the years, I have asked for many things.
But to all who hear my voice today,
Jesus is the way, the truth, and the life.
He is all you need for Christmas.

CHRISTMAS THOUGHTS

As I lay in my bed on Christmas night,
I thought about a baby born to bring light.
Into a world filled with darkness.
I thought about a little boy who came to bring me happiness,
And how He gave me more than just happiness; He gave me joy.
I thought about how blessed Mary felt when she held Her baby boy.
And how she must have given thanks to God above.
For giving birth to this baby who had nothing but love
To share with a world full of sinners.
I thought about my heavenly Father and how He must have felt,
sending His only begotten son to die to pay our debt.
I thought about how God loved this world
and sent His precious son to die to prove it.
I thought about ways of showing Him, my love.
I will accept His only son He sent from above.

A PRECIOUS GIFT

Who could have given a gift so wonderful?
A precious gift that would save the world,
A gift that is priceless and free,
One that God gave to you and me.

A precious gift we didn't have to buy,
but one who has bought us for a price.
A gift that was born to give His life,
That precious gift is Jesus Christ.

Please consider accepting this gift.
If you do not, you will lose eternal life.
It is God's gift to us from above,
One that He truly gave out of love.

MARY, MOTHER OF JESUS

Oh, how blessed was Mary,
To be chosen to carry the holy baby.
When the angel spoke to Mary,
She listened and obeyed.

God could have chosen any woman.
To carry and care for His only son.
He wanted someone humble and meek,
Someone strong in faith and not weak.

Mary, how you cared for Him throughout His life,
Always loving Him and doing what was right.
What an honor it must have been
To have given birth to the one who was free of sin.

JOSEPH, A WISE MAN

An angel spoke to a man named Joseph one night in a dream.
He was a bit confused and wondered to himself, *what does this mean?*
Joseph, being a wise man, realized it was a message from God.
He listened, obeyed, and did what he was told.
At times he thought about what people in the town would say
Because Mary was with a child, he had to marry her anyway.
Joseph, being a wise man, followed God's command.
Because he truly understood and wanted to be part of God's plan.

Just like Mary, he knew she would give birth to our Savior.
Joseph realized why God had shown her great favor.
She was a woman with wisdom, humility, and understanding,
Who was loved by God and Joseph, a wise man.

AN INNOCENT BABY

We all were born innocent babies.
But there was something special about baby Jesus.
It is because He was born to live and then die for us,
and for that reason, we can rejoice and be glad He was born.

An innocent baby who was born because of God's mercy,
He wanted to show the world just how much he cared.
What a blessing, an innocent baby for all to share.
Please accept Christ in your heart today.

Do not harden your heart and forget this innocent baby,
One who came so you could have life more abundantly.
God the Father loved us so much
He was willing to give His only son Jesus.

For God promised if you love Him with all your heart,
He will abide in us and will never depart.
Christ is the only answer for the world today.
Let Him love and adore you in His unique way.

Children, do you think innocent babies grow up and disobey their parents?
No, because we know that He was born without sin.
Can you all search your heart from deep within?
Do you listen to your parents now and then?

Or can you tell God that you have always obeyed?
We know that Christ obeyed His Father.
Christ is not happy with children who don't obey.
Please obey your parents, for Christ watches you each day.
God bless you.

WELCOME HIS BIRTH

From the beginning, God knew we would need a Savior.
He loved us and wanted to show us favor.
God sent His only son to be born on this Earth.
Christ, we love you, and we welcome your birth.

God loved us and did not want death to be our fate.
He sent His son to be born in a world full of hate.
He knew Christ would suffer and die on the cross.
Why not accept Him? He has already paid the cost.

He came that you and I may have a choice.
If He lives in your heart, be happy and rejoice,
and know that eternal life is yours if you believe.
Christ was once dead, but today He lives.

JESUS CAME TO GIVE US HOPE

Before the birth of our Lord and Savior,
we were lost, and it showed in our behavior.
Today we know if we believe,
We have hope and are not bound by chains and ropes.

Christ came to set us free and take our sins away.
If you will accept Him and live for Him each day,
You will be blessed with an abundance of love,
Sent down by our heavenly Father from above.

Christ is the hope that He came to give.
Though He died, yet he lives.
If we believe with all our hearts,
He will give us hope and a fresh start.

JESUS IS WAITING

Jesus is waiting with open arms.
Come to Him; He will do you no harm.
He yearns to love and hold you tight.
Let Him, and you will see the light.
Jesus is waiting; please give Him a chance.
Do not turn your back and walk away.
Just listen to what He has to say.
If you do, your life will not be such a mess.
When you accept Christ, you will gain eternal rest.

MARY'S SAVIOR TOO

One would have thought when Mary gave birth to Christ,
She would have done all she could to save His life.
But before Christ was conceived, Mary knew the reason for His birth.
She knew why God allowed His only son to be born on this Earth.

The angels told her God had shown her favor
Mary knew she would bring forth a son whose name would be Jesus.
A son of the Most High God, who would be called our Savior.
Mary knew He would be King of all Kings and would reign forever.

In her spirit, she rejoiced in God, her Savior.
She knew she was blessed among all women.
God chose her to give birth to Christ, who would rule forever.
Mary accepted her blessing from God, who has everything in His hands.

God chose Mary to be Christ's mother, but Christ was Mary's Savior too.
She gave birth to the holy baby, but He is the only one who can save you.

KING JESUS

To this King, my heart I bring.
To this King, a happy song I sing.
To this King, I will bow down and worship.
To this King, I will give thanks.
To this King, I will do a holy dance.
To this King, I will give a happy shout.
To this King, I know what you are about.
You are King Jesus, without a doubt.

A TALK WITH CHRIST

Christ, my Lord, and Savior, you came right on time.
What a good feeling, knowing you came to be mine.
When I heard about your amazing birth, Christ.
It filled my heart with joy because I knew you came to pay the price.
I was lost in sins and did not know where to turn.
Now that you have come, I will not have to burn in Hell.
Christ, if I can only get others to listen to me,
Then they will understand that you came to save the world.
I will not give up; I will get them to see.
You were born to set them free.

IF YOU LOVE CHRIST, SHARE THE GOOD NEWS

You said that you loved Jesus Christ
And you were glad He came into your life.
You also said that you were delighted He was born.
And would live your life for Him and Him alone.

Have you told Christ lately that you love Him?
And you would do all you can to share the good news?
For Christ did not come to save only you.
Go out and share the news; start with one or two.

You must be faithful to Christ and remain true.
Let others know they do not have to walk around feeling blue.
Christ was born on that wintry night.
So that they, too, could receive His precious light.

A PLACE NOT FIT FOR A KING

Joseph and Mary were in town one day.
To take care of business, not to stay.
While they were there, the time had come.
Mary to give birth to the holy one.
They went to an inn for a room.
It was then they learned there were no more.
I can imagine they were in shock, with no place to go.
The innkeeper told them about an old stable next door.
Joseph took Mary in and laid her on the floor.
Hours later, our Lord and Savior was born.
They had no place for Him to lay His head.
Joseph found a manger and filled it with hay.
Mary wrapped Him in swaddling clothes,
and there in the manger, our Savior lay,
Born in a place not fit for a King.

HALLELUJAH

H is for hallelujah; Christ was born.

A is for the angels that watched over Him.

L is for the love He came to give to us.

L is for the light we can see because He came.

E is for the everlasting life He was born to give.

L is for the Lord; He is called Lord of Lords.

U is for the understanding He brings to the world.

J is for Jesus, who was born for you and me.

A is for the Almighty, born with all power in His hands.

H is for hallelujah; a Savior was born.

HE IS COMING BACK

Some people believe Christ never died on the cross,
So how could He come back to life?
Some people say He is not a Savior,
They say He is just a man.
To whom God showed favor.
But I stand before you today.
To tell you Christ died on the cross,
and He arose on the third day.
If you do not believe He did, your soul is lost.
Christ is returning for me and all who accept Him.

MY THANKS TO CHRIST

Christ, I thank you for what you did.
When you were nailed to the cross.
You did exactly what you said.
You took my sins along with you.
Christ, I thank you because,
dying on the cross, you did not have to do,
But you did it anyway,
because of the love you have for me.
And you want to see me in Heaven one day.
Thank you, Christ, for dying in such a sad way.

A MOTHER'S LOVE

She must have felt such joy.
To have given birth to a baby boy.
Mary knew it was a gift sent from above,
and she felt the goodness of a mother's love.

A mother's love is always caring,
Never selfish and always willing to share.
Mary shared Jesus with the world.
Because she knew one day, He would save us all.

A mother's love means tears of joy.
Mary shed them when she held her baby boy.
She thanked God, who had shown her favor,
For Mary knew He was born to be our Savior.

I will come again.

CHRIST IS ALIVE AND WAITING FOR YOU

Christ is alive and waiting for you with open arms.
He wants you to trust and believe in Him; He will do you no harm.
He yearns for you to do what is right and not succumb to Satan's temptations.
Christ wants to give you the gift of Salvation.

With us, He wants a personal relationship.
Just talk to Him, pray to Him, love Him, and do not wait; do it.
It is not Christ's desire for any of us to die and go to Hell.
He commands us to abide in Him and to do good as well.

I can imagine Him sitting at the right hand of God the Father.
With tears in His eyes because some of us don't want to be bothered.
Christ died to show us His unchanging love.
Will you accept Him in your heart today and be blessed from above?

MARY'S BROKEN HEART

Mary stood near the cross with tears in her eyes.
She watched in disbelief as Christ died.
She knew that for the world, this was a new start.
But nothing could heal Mary's, broken heart.
I can imagine she cried out, "Please help my son."
In her heart, she knew the reason He had been born.
She realized this was the day He had to die.
But nothing could be said to heal Mary's broken heart.

THINGS CHRIST MAY HAVE SAID TO HIS FATHER

Father, I love you, and it is you I want to please.
I prayed to you, Father, and this is the answer I received.
Yes, Father, I will go to the cross and give my life.
Because I know this is your holy and divine will.
I will listen and obey because I know this is right.
And when I return, the world will see me as their light.
For if I do not obey you, my precious Father,
How can I expect the world to choose me to follow?

JESUS IS WITH ME

When I get up in the morning,
Jesus is there, and He asks how I am doing.
When I get on the bus to go to school,
He sits next to me and tells me I am blessed.
When I get to my classroom
and my teacher is having a difficult day,
Jesus, you can tell her you are the way.
When I get home and start my homework,
Jesus tells me I can do it because I am smart.
And when I kneel to say my prayers at night,
He tells me He loves me and to sleep tight.

CHRIST, CAN YOU WALK WITH ME?

My burdens are heavy and unbearable sometimes.
People laugh and tell me I am out of my mind.
Christ died on the cross for me.
They say I am silly for believing, and how could that be?
Sometimes I feel like I am all alone.
Why can't people believe what Christ has done?
Christ, my heart is heavy; can you walk with me?
Thank you because you died to set you free."

CHRIST'S WALK TO THE CROSS

The crowd grew larger, and the line got longer.
One can only imagine how lonely Christ must have felt.
His walk to the cross was painful, and He had little help.
He had to carry His cross on His back.
Christ never complained, and no questions did He ask.
I know His walk to the cross was not an easy one.
Some in the crowd were angry, some glad, and some mourned.
He was beaten severely and scorned.
But Christ remained obedient, never forgetting why He was born.

CHRIST'S THOUGHTS
ON THE CROSS

As I looked around at the people in the crowd,
I saw some who were sad and some who were proud.
Oh, no, and there is my mother with tears in her eyes.
Mother, please do not cry because you know why.
My heavenly Father said I must die.
He wants to save a world He cares so much for.
Therefore, I must die for the world.

HE CAME BACK TO LIFE.

Jesus was once dead.
I saw Him when He hung His head.
Three days later, He came back to life.
He was among His people for a while.
Then He ascended back into Heaven.
To prepare a place for all who believe
That He was once dead but came back to life.

IF I COULD HAVE
CARRIED HIS CROSS

Christ was beaten brutally all night long.
The following day, He was kicked and beaten again.
How can they do all these things to an innocent man?
Next, they put on his head a crown made of thorns.
Then He was given His cross to carry alone.
Christ, if I could, I would have carried your cross.
Then they led Him down a road and up Calvary's hill.
Seeing all of this made it hard for me to stand still.
Christ, I am sad and hurt by what you went through.
If I could have carried your cross, I would have.

CHRIST OBEYED HIS FATHER

Christ faithfully prayed in the garden that night.
He wanted to be sure He heard His Father's voice right.
He asked His Father to take the cup away
After many hours of praying in The garden
After many hours of praying, He received the answer
He listened and obeyed His Father

PEACE, LOVE, AND JOY

Christ has peace; I have peace.
Christ has love; I have love.
Christ has joy; I have joy.
Thank you, Jesus Christ.
You have made me a happy boy.

I WATCHED, AND I LISTENED

Christ, I listened to you pray.
Christ, I listened to you teach.
Christ, I listened to your stories.

Christ, I watched as you carried.
Your cross up a hill so high.
Christ, I watched you as you died.
And I watched as you ascended back to Heaven.

CHRIST WILL RETURN

Even though Christ may ascend and go away,
He will return for us one day.
Do not be sad and heavily burdened,
and do not let your heart be hardened.
For He will go away to prepare a place.
Oh, what joy we will have when we see His face,
When He return to gather His faithful sheep.

STOP BEATING HIM

I stood in the back of the crowd.
I saw them beat Him until He fell to the ground.
He got up and was beaten to His knees.
I heard a voice say, "Stop beating Him, please."
I moved from the back to a different place.
I wanted to see my Savior's face.
His body was bloody, battered, and bruised.
I cried to them, "Stop beating Him, please."
By then, my Lord and Savior were tired and weak.
But He continued to walk up Calvary's hill.
Because He knew this was His Father's will.

CHRIST IS ALWAYS WITH ME

When I wake up in the morning, He is by my side.
Christ is with me at school, and I cannot hide His love.
When I sit down to bless and eat my lunch,
I know He is with me, and I must thank Him.

When others talk about me and do terrible things to me, I am not afraid,
because Christ is with me and He will protect me, He said.
When I go to bed, I pray to Him at night,
I know He will lead and guide me to do what is right.

I WISH

When I say I have a Savior,
I wish people would believe me.
When I say Christ died on the cross,
I wish they wouldn't laugh,
and say that it is false.
I wish when Christ comes back for me,
That they would see I was telling the truth.
I wish that it wouldn't be too late.
But I know, for some, it will be,
and they won't enter Heaven.

CAN I SEE YOUR HANDS?

I heard about a man.
Who was nailed to a cross,
A man who died in agony and pain.
I did not believe it, as I was thinking,
What did He have to gain?
As I was walking down a road,
I heard one person say to another,
"There is the man who died and arose.
There was something different about this man.
So, I asked Him, 'Can I see your hands?'
He showed His hands to me.
There were holes I could see.
Now all I could say was,
'I believe! I believe! I believe!'

HE IS ALL YOU NEED

Christ is my life.
Christ is my friend.
Christ is my Savior.
Christ is able.
To do all things.
If you put your trust in Him,
He is all you need.

PRIDE

Before Christ died
I was lost in my pride.
I did not need a Savior.
Why go to the cross for me?
I have money; that is all I need.
I do not need anything for free.

But now I realize how wrong I was.
For thinking in such a foolish way.
Christ died to save me from my sins,
Something I surely cannot do on my own.

Now that I know I cannot save myself,
The pride I had is gone.

PRAY IN JESUS' NAME

Christ, when I am sad,
and things are not going right,
It gives me comfort.
To know when I say
my prayers at night,
I can pray in your name and
You will make everything right.

HE LISTENS

When I talk to Christ,
He always listens to me.
Because He knows my heart,
and He knows that He is first
in my life.
Thank you, Christ,
for always listening
to what I have to say.

I WILL FOLLOW YOU FOREVER

Christ, I have never been one to follow.
I have always wanted to be a leader.
Now I realize since I have accepted you,
That you have the right to tell me what to do.
I have peace in being a follower.
Now that I know that you will be my leader,
I will follow you forever.

THERE IS JOY IN KNOWING CHRIST

Throughout my life, I have had some happiness.
I have had some good days, and some were bad.
Whatever I did, I gave it my best.
Now I realize some of my choices were not good.
But today, I can be happy and rejoice,
Because one day, I heard a voice,
Jesus wamts me to follow because He is my Savior.
If you follow Him I will have joy.
Today I know there is joy in knowing Christ.

CHRIST IS

Christ is our Lord and only Savior.
Christ is the one who asked God to show us favor.
Christ is the righteousness and goodness; He came to teach.
Christ is our innocent Savior, whose love we seek.
Christ is our Lord, the one who is strong and not weak.
Christ is a teacher who taught us to love one another.
Christ is merciful and shows it to us in a unique way.
Christ is the one who abides in us each day.
Christ is the Shepherd whose sheep know His voice.
Christ is always with us, and for this, we can rejoice.
Christ is our only intercessor; His promises He keeps.
Christ is the one who never leaves His sheep.
Christ is the only hope for the world today.

A Play

Nina's Love for Jesus

Cast

Two Girls Aged 12 or 13,

Two Boys Aged 12 or 13,

One Girl 11 (Nina's Sister)

Two Adults Male (Fathers),

Two Adult Females (Mothers)

And lots of extras for the church congregation and choir. You will also need a preacher to preach a 5–10-minute sermon on the death and Resurrection of Jesus.

Scene One

(In the school cafeteria during lunch, Nina is sitting with four of her friends)

Nina

(Sits down at the table)

Hi guys, what are you all discussing? From the looks on your faces, it is intense.

Jimmy

(While giggling)

We are talking about Easter, and Larry is saying some weird things about what he and his family do for Easter.

Nina

What do you mean,?

Jimmy

He is talking about going to church and somebody named Jesus, who died and came back alive.

Nicole

Yes, he is scaring me; who dies for someone? And get this; then he said, this Jesus comes back alive. *(While giggling)*

Nina

Jesus Did!

Jimmy

I am not the only weird one; Nina believes the same; she and I have talked about this before.

Nina

Larry and Nicole, what do you all do on Easter Sunday?

Larry

"We do nothing! It is just another day. We do what we usually do. My dad washes his cars, and my mom goes shopping and gets her hair and nails done. I play video games and watch TV. That is easy.

Nicole

In my house, the night before, the Easter bunny comes while we are asleep to bring my sister and me candy and other things, just like on Christmas when Santa Claus comes and brings us the things we asked for because we weren't naughty but nice.

Jimmy

(He and Nina have a look of disbelief on their face)

Do you mean neither of your families believes in or celebrates Jesus's birth, death, and Resurrection?

Nina

Yes, celebrating Jesus is all I know. I may get some candy or go to an Easter egg hunt, but first, we celebrate Jesus.

Jimmy

The same happens in our house also. My father will not have it any other way.

Nicole

Oh, yes! We do the egg hunt too. We also go to church but don't make a big deal; just like Christmas, we go to church, but gifts are the most important thing.

Nina

Nicole, I also get gifts on Christmas, but the most important gift I ever received is the gift of salvation, and my parents didn't pay any money for this gift.

Jimmy

Me too; the day I received the gift of salvation was the best day of my life. Anyone can receive this gift anytime; there is no special day to get it.

Nina

Yes, a person must want it, and Jesus will give it.

Larry

Yall lives are boring; who goes to church and spends half the day there when they could be having fun?

Nicole

Yes! That sounds odd to me; come on, Larry, let's go to class; the bell is about to ring. (Larry and Nicole walk away.)

Nina

I do not understand why parents aren't teaching their children about Jesus and what He did on the cross. Nicole and Larry don't know the truth.

Jimmy

Yes, it is their parents' fault because they are not teaching them.

Nina

When I accepted Jesus, I deeply fell in love with Him because of what He did for me. It is personal to me. **Jimmy**, I love him so much, and it hurts me when people don't care to know Him and the real reason we celebrate Easter.

Jimmy

Yes, I know the feeling; we will continue to try and get them to come around. So, we pray for them.

Nina

Let's pray now.

Jimmy

Sounds good,

Nina

(They held hands and prayed) Father God, we pray you will touch Larry's and Nicole's hearts. Father God, we pray you will touch their parents' hearts to teach them the truth about Jesus. We love You, Father God. We pray this prayer in Jesus's name. Amen,

(Nina and Jimmy leave for class)

Lights out.

Scene Two

(Setting, at Nina's home during dinner)

Mother

Nina, how was school today?

Nina

It was ok, Mom **(Nina speaking sadly)**

Father

What is wrong, Nina? You do not seem happy,

Sister

Yes, she has been shut in her room since she came home from school.

Nina

I do not understand why others don't love Jesus as I do.

Father

Nina, honey, when people don't know someone, it is hard to love that person.

Nina

Yes, but I just don't get it. Why don't parents teach their children about Jesus and what He did on the cross for us?

Mother

It is because they are lost. Therefore, they can't teach what they don't know.

Sister

Yes, Nina, don't feel bad because I talked about Easter and why we celebrate it; everyone laughed at me. I felt sad for them.

Nina

Yes, Jimmy and I felt sad, too; we prayed for them when Larry and Nicole left.

Mother

Doesn't Larry's mother have cancer? I worked with his father, and he shared it with us.

Nina

Oh, no, Mom! Larry has not mentioned it to me.

Sister

So, his mother can die without Jesus? Mom, Dad that would not be good. We must do something.

Father

We pray for them.

Mother

Yes, because I have talked to Larry's father about Jesus, but he refuses to speak to me about religion.

Father

When this happens, we can't take it personal. People are not rejecting us; they are rejecting Jesus. I know this is sad, but it is the truth.

Nina

It is God's will that everyone come to Heaven when they die,

Father

Yes, this is true; this is why He sent His son Jesus to the cross to die for our sins.

Mother

Yes, we pray.

Nina

Jimmy, Larry, Nicole, and I are best friends. It saddens me to know that they are lost.

Sister

Nina, I know how you feel. People mock me when they see me coming. They mocked Jesus too.

Father

Yes, girls, as Christians, we are going to be mocked. We are going to be talked about and persecuted. We must be strong for Jesus.

Mother

Yes, sometimes we are sent to plant the seed, and someone else will come and water it, then God gives the increase.

Nina

(She gets emotional and says)

So, we just let Larry's mother die without Jesus?

Sister

No, Nina, this is not what Mom and Dad mean; they said we are to pray for them, just like you and Jimmy did today.

Father

You just said it is not God's will for anyone to die without His son. When we can't reach people by sharing Jesus, we pray. Now please, honey, eat your dinner.

Nina

I am not hungry.

(She gets up and walks away from the table, the scene ends with the father, mother, and sister praying as the lights go out)

Scene Three

(Setting, at Larry's home, the family is having breakfast when his mother passes out and is rushed to the hospital)

Larry

Mama, you do not look well today. Are you ok?

Mother

No, Larry, I am not feeling well. I did not rest well last night.

Father

No son, she tossed and turned all night.

Larry

Dad, what is wrong with her? I know you have all been keeping something from me.

Father

She has some issues, but the doctors say she will be ok.

Larry

But how can she be? She never eats anything, and she is losing so much weight. Last night she did not sit at the table with us. (He raises his voice)

Father

Son, she will be fine. *(He raises his voice and points his finger at Larry)* Don't you raise your voice in this house again!

Larry

(While pushing his chair back, getting ready to leave)

I am sick of all these secrets; I am going to bed.

Mother

No, please, Larry, don't leave. Sit down.

Father

No, let him leave, and while he is gone, he can stay in his room until he learns some respect.

(Father and son are angry and going back and forth with each other.)

Mother

(Yells)

Stop it, please! Sit down, Larry. You should know.

Larry

Know what, mama?

Father

Yes, son, please sit down.

Mother

(She appears to be very weak)

Son, I am dying; I have breast cancer.

Larry

What? Why didn't you tell me, mama?

Mother

Son, we didn't want you to worry and fall behind on your schoolwork.

Father

Yes, son, we thought it best that you didn't know.

Mother

I decided not to tell you because you are my only child, and I do not want to see you hurting.

Larry

(While crying)

But Mama, you can't die; please don't die. What will Dad and I do without you?

Mother

Don't cry, son; your father will take care of you. I will be ok. Also, you will have your grandmothers and aunts. They will be there for you.

(Larry gets up and hugs his mother while crying, his mother cries while telling him that things will be ok.)

Father

Son, we will be ok; get yourself ready for school. Your mother has an appointment to have surgery.

Larry

Surgery?

Mother

Yes, son, they will remove the cancerous breast.

Larry

Mother, I cannot go to school knowing you are having surgery. I must go with you.

Father

Son, I think you should go to school.

Mother

It is ok if he comes to the hospital with us. I think he should be there.

Father

Ok!

(Mother was getting up from the table and passed out. Father holds mother and tells Larry to call EMS. Larry is hysterical, but he calls 911.)

Lights out.

Scene Four

(Setting at the hospital waiting room. Larry calls Nina and tells her what is going on.)

Nina

(Her phone rings, and she puts the phone on speaker so the audience can hear.)

Hi Larry, I thought you were mad at me because of the way you left yesterday.

Larry

No, I am tired of the Jesus stuff you and Jimmy always discuss.

Nina

I will not apologize to you because God wants all to know about His son.

Larry

Yeah! Enough about that Jesus stuff. My mother is dying.

Nina

What do you mean?

Larry

My mother told me that she has cancer.

Nina

I know, but cancer is not a death sentence. My mother mentioned this when we were talking last night.

Larry

She had it for a long time; they kept it from me. They told others because now I am learning that you knew.

Nina

Yes, my mother found out at work. I am so sorry Larry. Why are you calling me this early? I am getting ready for school.

Larry

I am at the hospital. My mother passed out while we were having breakfast.

Nina

OH NO, Larry! Is she ok?

Larry

We don't know; the nurse took her straight to the back. She mentioned something about shallow breathing. I do not know what that means.

Nina

Hmmm, that does not sound good. I will tell my mother what is happening and have her drop me off at the hospital.

Larry

Sounds excellent, Nina, because I am scared.

Nina

It is ok; you are my friend. Oh, what hospital?

Larry

Hopewell

Nina

Ok, I will see you in about ten minutes.

(Meanwhile, the doctor told Larry and his father that his mother didn't make it.)

Larry

(While pushing the doctor.)

What do you mean she didn't make it?

Father

(He grabbed his son and hugged him as they both cried)

It is ok, son. We will get through this together.

Larry

But Dad, she is gone; it will not be all right. It will never be ok.

(Nina walks in during all the commotions)

Nina

Larry, what is wrong? Why are you crying?

Larry

(Hugs, Nina)

My mother is gone, Nina. She is dead! What would I do without her? I do not want to live.

Nina

Larry, I am so sorry; it is going to be ok. Your mother would want you to live your life. Come on and sit down.

(Nina gets a tissue from her purse and gives it to Larry)

Nina

(Ask Larry's father)

Mr. Johnson, are you ok? I am so sorry.

Father

Yes, Nina, it is hard, but I will be fine. I am worried about Larry; we told him this morning. He learned about his mother's breast cancer this morning. Her death is a total shock to him.

Nina

Do not worry; I will help him. Mr. Johnson, may I ask you a question.

Father

Yes, Nina, what is it?

Nina

Larry tells me that you all do not believe in Jesus. Is this true?

Father

Nina, it is partially true.

Nina

Hmmm, I do not understand.

Father

Well, when his mother and I met, she was a Christian. She knew I was not. She loved and married me anyway.

Nina

Interesting, I knew there was peace about her. Why haven't you and Larry accepted Christ?

Father

After we were married, I told her that I did not want my son raised as a Christian and that she could not talk about Jesus ever in front of him. She honored my wishes.

Nina

Oh, wow! That is deep, so this explains Larry's attitude when I talk about Jesus to him.

Father

Yes, and now I wonder if that was the right choice because she had peace, even knowing she was dying.

Nina

Yes, Jesus gives peace that only Christians can understand.

Father

Yes, I saw it in her. Now, looking at my son losing his mother, he has no peace, I have no peace,

Nina

But Mr. Johnson, it is not too late. Easter is a week away. Will you and Larry come to our Easter service?

Father

I will think about it. Where do you go to church?

Nina

The Vine Baptist Church.

(Nina and Larry's father went over to hug Larry.)

Lights out.

Scene Five

(Setting, before school in the cafeteria after the passing and burial of Larry's mother. Larry sat down at the table.)

Nicole

Hi Larry, it is good to see you. I am so sorry about the passing of your mother.

Jimmy

Yes, Larry, when Nina called and told me, I was shocked because I did not know your mother was ill.

Larry

The sad thing is, I did not know either.

Nicole

What do you mean, Larry?

Larry

Exactly what I said, I did not find out until the morning my mother died.

Nina

It was because your parents didn't want you to worry while doing schoolwork.

Jimmy

Yes, they thought they were doing what was best for you.

Larry

(Breaks down sobbing)
But if they had told me, I could have been prepared for her passing.

Nina

Yes, I understand what you are saying, but mentally we are never prepared to lose our loved ones.

Jimmy

Larry, is it ok if we pray with you?

Larry

No, I do not want to hear about that Jesus person today. If He cared about me, why did He take my mother?

Nina

Please, calm down. Jesus does love you. He did not take your mother's life because He was angry but because He loves her.

Jimmy

Yes, He did not want her to suffer anymore.

Nicole

So, where did his mother's soul go?

Nina

Her soul is in Heaven.

Nicole

(Smartly says)

But how because they didn't believe in God?

Nina

Nicole, can you please be more considerate in asking your questions?

Nicole

Yes, whatever!

Larry

Is her soul in Heaven? Nina, how do you know this? Are you God?

Nina

No, Larry, I am not God. However, while you were sitting last night, I got to talk to your father about Jesus.

Larry

Did you?

Nina

Yes, I did.

Jimmy

Wow, Nina, you did?

Nina

Yes, and I found out that your mother was a Christian.

Larry

Was she? But she nor my father ever talked about God.

Nina

It is because when your father and mother married, she was a Christian, but your father was not. When she was pregnant with you, your mother told him not to talk to you about Jesus.

Nicole

That is whack!

Nina

He wanted you to grow up and make your own choice.

Larry

Oh, wow! I never knew this. So, this is why I have all these issues.

Nicole

Yes, just like me.

Jimmy

No, Nicole, there is nothing wrong with either of you. Your parents didn't train you all up, but this is not you and Larry's fault.

Nina

Yes, you are going to be ok. Larry, I invited your father and you to our Easter service.

Larry

And what did He say?

Nina

He said he would consider it, but I believe you and your father will attend church on Easter Sunday. Looking at him, I saw a concerned look on his face.

Jimmy

I will be there. Also, Nicole, why don't you join us too,

Nina

I am looking forward to seeing all of you in church.

(The bell rings, and they all leave)

Lights out.

Scene Six

(Conclusion)

(Setting at church will need an area like a church setting, a small or big choir, and a preacher. The preacher will also do an invitation after the sermon. Larry, his father, Nicole, and her family (Her father, mother, brother, and sister), therefore many extras are needed. The preacher can lead the group in a prayer of salvation, repentance, and forgiveness. Nina is waiting in the church foyer while her parents and sister go into the church)

(Nina is walking the floor, then she hears a voice)

Nicole

Hi Nina!

Nina

Hi Nicole, I am so glad to see you.

Nicole

My parents, sister, and brother came too.

Nina

Awesome! Oh, and there is Jimmy.

Nicole

Hi Jimmy!

Jimmy

Hi Nicole and Nina

(They spoke to Jimmy)

Jimmy

Did you see Larry and his father?

Nina

No, they are not here.

Jimmy

It is 10:00, and service is about to start.

Nina

Well, we tried.

Nicole

They are running late.

Nicole

Oh! Here they come.

Nina

(Walks over and greets them)

Hi, and welcome to The Vine Baptist Church.

Larry's Father

Thank you for inviting us. We are glad to be here.

Nina

Excellent, I felt in my heart that you all would come. Service is starting; let's go inside.

(Short service, scripture and prayer, a couple of worship songs, then a sermon on the death and Resurrection of our Lord and Savior. Then the invitation.) Larry, his father, and Nicole accepted Jesus as Savior and Lord.

(After service, the four friends are standing in the foyer.}

Nina

So, Nicole and Larry, how do you all feel?

Larry

Good, I have peace about my mother's death.

Nicole

I feel peaceful also.

Nina

And now the angels in Heaven are having a party. God is smiling. And all I can say is PRAISE THE LORD!

Larry

Group hug!

Lights out

SCRIPTURES TO ASSIST IN LEADING SOMEONE TO CHRIST.

[16] "For God so loved the world that He gave His only begotten Son, that whoever believes in Him should not perish but have everlasting life."

John 3:16 (NKJV)

[6] "Jesus said to him, "I am the way, the truth, and the life. No one comes to the Father except through Me."

John 14:6 (NKJV)

[23] "for all have sinned and fall short of the glory of God."

Romans 3:23 (NKJV)

[23] "For the wages of sin *is* death, but the [a]gift of God *is* eternal life in Christ Jesus our Lord."

Romans 6:23 (NKJV)

[9] "That if you confess with your mouth the Lord Jesus and believe in your heart that God has raised Him from the dead, you will be saved. [10] For with the heart one believes unto righteousness, and with the mouth, confession is made unto salvation."

Romans 10:9-10 (NKJV)

[12] "Nor is there salvation in any other, for there is no other name under heaven given among men by which we must be saved."

Acts 4:12 (NKJV)

The church that presents this play will gain God's favor.
I pray this drama is blessed in Jesus's name.
Amen

MARY'S DESIRE FOR ALL TO KNOW JESUS

Characters Needed for the Play

(Two Families)

(Consist of two girls aged 14 or 15, two fathers, two mothers, two boys aged 14 or 15, a teacher, a principal, a grandmother, a preacher, and extra children and adults for the congregation, choir, and the classroom.)

The Play

Scene One

(Setting in the home of an unsaved family except for the daughter, they are having breakfast)

Father

This is the best breakfast you have ever cooked, honey,

Mother

I know; I used a unique ingredient in the eggs today.

Mary

Yes, Dad, the food is good, but what about praying over our food?

Father

What do you mean by praying over food? Who is telling you to pray over your food?

Jimmy

Yes, she has been acting weird ever since she became friends with the holy girl.

Mary

Well, I am not a wannabe gang member!

Jimmy

(yelling) It is better than following someone who talks about Jesus all the tine!

Father

Wait a minute; what is going on? You two had better stop before I punish both of you.

Mother

Yes, what is wrong with you, Mary? You know we do not do the Jesus thing in this house. God and prayer get us nothing, so why believe?

Father

Yes, I am the head of this house, and I say what we do and do not do, who we talk about, and do not talk about; this is a warning, Mary!

Mother

I cannot believe that Christmas will be here in a month, and you all are acting like this.

Father

Yes, if the two of you keep it up, I will take back the twenty-five gifts each of you have under the Christmas tree.

Mother

Yes, I agree with your father.

Mary

Mom and dad, this is not what Christmas is all about. God sent His only son Jesus to be born in a cruel and evil world where His mother gave birth to Him in a stable, a place not fit for royalty.

Jimmy

Mom, please do not take any of my gifts back. Mary knows we get all these gifts yearly, and now she wants to replace them with someone she cannot see. She is saying some weird things. Please take all her gifts back and buy me more.

Mary

Yes, but my friend Diane says that Christmas is about giving, but not like how we celebrate; she says it is all about Jesus's birth. There is nothing wrong with giving and receiving gifts, but we cannot forget the ultimate gift God gave the world, His son Jesus Christ.

Father

(Stands up yelling) Now look, Mary, stop it; I do not want to hear another word about Jesus, God, and other names you call Him. In this house, we do not talk about people we cannot see. People are just spreading lies and more lies.

Jimmy

Yeah, you tell her dad! I am tired of hearing this nonsense; also, a baby to save the world, yeah, right! How can she fall for this untruth?

Mary

(*Yelling at her brother*) Be quiet and leave me alone; I hate you. Mom and Dad always take your side; I pray you will know and accept the truth one day.

Jimmy

That is because you think you are better than us and do not hold your breath; I will not believe in this Jesus person. He will not steal Christmas.

Mother

Jimmy and Mary, stop it! Enough is enough; anyway, the school bus will be here soon. Go and finish getting ready.
(*The two leave the room*)

Mother

What is wrong with Mary? She has been acting a little weird over the last few months. I found a book called Bible under her bed.

Father

I will get rid of it; this is the book those so call Christians live by; it is all a bunch of lies.

(*Mom and Dad leave for work*)

Lights out.

Scene Two

(Setting in Mary's classroom at school, the director will need extra students for this setting. The teacher walks into the classroom)

Teacher

Good morning

Class (All except Mary)

Good morning, Ms. Johnson

Teacher

Did you all complete your homework?
(The class responded yes, except Mary; she sat with her head down on her desk.)

Class

Yes, Ms. Johnson

Teacher

Okay, pass your homework to the front of the class,
(Everyone did except Mary. Ms. Johnson walked over to Mary's desk and asked if there was a problem.)

Teacher

What is the problem? You always have your homework. "What's wrong?"

Mary

(*yells*) Nothing! I am tired of my boring, and odd family; they do not believe in God or pray over their food. We celebrate Christmas by giving all these gifts in my house, but no one talks about Jesus. (All the children laughed at Mary except Diane, and this angers her)

Teacher

Mary, there is no need to yell; Christmas is about giving gifts, singing songs, and spending time with family. Besides, Jesus is not real, and we do not discuss religion in school.

Mary

(Angrily says) So you believe like my family. Everyone wants Jesus out of Christmas when He is the reason for the season. You are odd, just like my family.

Teacher

Mary, you are out of control; I am sending you to the principal's office.

Mary

It is okay with me; he will know why we are supposed to celebrate Christmas, and yes, I am out of control for Jesus! (*Mary grabs her things and runs out of the classroom*)

(*Mary arrives in the principal's office upset; the principal asked her to have a seat*)

Principal

Mary, you are the last person I expected *to see in my office today. What is going on?*

Mary

I am sorry; this day started badly for me at home.

Principal

What do you mean? Do you need to talk to the counselor? She is there for students when they need to talk.

Mary

No, I do not.

Principal

You should be excited; school is getting out for Christmas break soon.

Mary

This is part of the problem; my family does not know the real reason for Christmas, which frustrates me. They do not believe, and Ms. Johnson does not believe either.

Principal

Believe what?

Mary

The real reason for Christmas,

Principal

What is it about Christmas that causes you to act out in class and can eventually get you expelled from school?

Mary

I am sorry; I will apologize to Ms. Johnson; Mr. Shaw, what do you believe about Christmas?

Principal

Christmas is a time to go shopping, give your family and friends gifts, put up lights and trees, roast marshmallows, and do fun stuff.

Mary

This is unbelievable; does anyone know the real reason for Christmas besides Diane, her family, and me?

Principal

I thought I did, but it was not the correct answer.

Mary

No, it is not, but it is okay. Let me go and apologize to Ms. Johnson, the class, and Mr. Shaw; I will pray for you. There will be a Christmas service at The Living God Church; I will pray that I see you there.

(The last bell rang, Mary left the office, returned to the classroom, and apologized to Ms. Johnson; Mary invited her to the Christmas service, and then she left.

Lights out.

Scene Three

(Setting, Diane is at home, she calls Mary, and each puts their phone on speaker so the audience can hear the conversation.)

Mary

(*Her phone rings*) Hello

Diane

What was that all about in the classroom?

Mary

What do you mean?

Diane

You were acting out and yelling at Ms. Johnson today.

Mary

I was frustrated; my family could not see that we were not celebrating Christmas the way I had learned from you and your family. My brother and I were arguing, and my father did not want to hear the truth.

Diane

I am sorry that your morning started roughly; your attitude was not how a Christian should act.

Mary

I know, Diane; I am sorry. I went back to say apologize but everyone had left.

Diane

What about Ms. Johnson?

Mary

She was still in the room; I told her I was sorry.

Diane

Have you told your parents you accepted Jesus as your Lord and Savior?

Mary

No, because every time I mention Jesus, my brother calls me names, and my father yells at me, telling me not to bring the God stuff into his house.

Diane

Oh my, he is going to be hard to reach. What about your mother?

Mary

My mother is the easiest out of the three of them.

Diane

That is good, Mary. Can you come over tomorrow after school?

Mary

Yes, I will ask my parents.

Diane

Okay, see you tomorrow in class.

Mary

Sounds good; wait a minute, Diane, why didn't you speak up for me today?

Diane

What do you mean?

Mary

You were in class today; you believe as I do; you should have spoken up and helped me defend Jesus.

Diane

Yes, and we would have gone to the principal's office together. Anyway, this is what I want to talk to you about tomorrow when you come over,

Mary

Okay, talk to you later.

Lights out.

Scene Four

(The home of the Christian family during dinner)

Father

Father God, we thank you for the food we are about to receive; may it be nourishment for our bodies to be healthy to further your kingdom here on earth. In Jesus's name, I pray.

All

Amen!

Mother

Diane, how was school today?

Diane

It was okay.

Mother

Hmmm, why just ok? Did you get into trouble today?

Diane

No, I did not, but Mary did.

Kevin

Mary got in trouble; who would have thought she would be in trouble?

Diane

Yes, she did, Kevin; I know you have a crush on her; I see how you look at her when she comes over.

Kevin

(As he smiles) Well, she is pretty.

Diane

Let us leave it at that, you and my best friend, no, I don't think so.

Father

What happened to Mary at school today?

Mother

Yes, what happened?

Diane

Ever since she accepted Christ and discovered the real reason for Christmas, she wants everybody to believe and accept Jesus.

Brother

What is wrong with her wanting people to know?

Father

Yes, we should all share the good news of Jesus and let people know our hope in Him.

Mother

Yes, this is true, but we must know how to share it with others.

Diane

Yes, mom, exactly! When the subject of Christmas came up today in class, Mary asked Ms. Johnson what she believed about Christmas.

Kevin

I hope she mentioned Jesus!

Diane

Will you be quiet and let me finish the story?

Kevin

Yeah! Okay! Whatever!

Diane

(As she rolled her eyes at her brother) When Mary discovered that Ms. Johnson did not believe Jesus was the reason for the season, she got angry and started yelling at Ms. Johnson.

Father

She did not manage the situation like a Christian.

Mother

No, she did not; we cannot make people believe in Jesus,

Diane

The worse part was when the children in the classroom laughed at her, which did not make matters better.

Kevin

(Smartly says) Did you defend her? She is your best friend.

Diane

(Raised her voice) No, I did not defend her; we were in the classroom. Besides, there is a way and a place to handle situations that involve Jesus.

Father

Yes, son, there is a proper way to do things as Christians.

Diane

I felt terrible when Ms. Johnson sent her to the principal's office.

Mother

Oh my, so things got a little out of hand.

Diane

Yes, they did,

Father

I am sorry this happened; she has not been a Christian long. Perhaps when she comes over again, we can speak with her about how Christians are supposed to manage complicated issues.

Diane

It has already been taken care of; she will come after school tomorrow.

Kevin

Cool! So, I get to see her tomorrow.

Diane

Yes, Kevin, but not to see you. Anyway, you are like a brother to her, so get over yourself.

Mother

Sounds excellent; Kevin, please do your homework; Diane, help me with the dishes.

Father

I am going to my office to prepare for the Sunday school lesson. We are continuing the study of the birth of Jesus.

Mother

Okay

(Lights out)

Scene Five

(Setting in the living room of Mary's home)

Mother

(Ask father about work today) How was work today?

Father

Just like every other day, working in the hospital wearing a mask is not easy. Seeing people come in sick and dying is not an easy job,

Mother

Yes, I know working in the medical field is not easy right now,

Father

Yes, five patients died today from the Covid-19, and we have patients with cancer, heart disease, and other sicknesses. It can be stressful.

Jimmy

I am sick of this virus and people dying, not to mention wearing these masks daily. I did not wear mine in the mall today.

Mary

What? Do you know you can get the virus and spread it to all of us?

Jimmy

I will not get it; I am healthy, and please do not start on me about this Jesus person. If He cared about us, why did He allow the virus to kill so many people?

Mary

Jimmy, not wearing a mask is not an intelligent thing to do. Why would you want to expose yourself to the virus?

Jimmy

My friends and I did a challenge. We want to prove this Jesus person wrong; He does not control everything.

Father

Jimmy, your sister is right; you will have to be test for the virus and put in quarantine because you did this.

Jimmy

Dad, please do not make me take this test. I am fifteen and too young to get Covid-19.

Fatherss

Son, you know my profession; I deal with this every day. The Pandemic is real. You must take the test, and you will have to stay in your room for a few days.

Mother

Yes, this is best for the family.

Jimmy

So, I cannot go to school or hang out with my boys?

Father

No, Jimmy! What you did was childish.

Mary

I will pray that you do not get it, Kevin.

Jimmy

Yeah right! (*He leaves the room*)

Mary

Dad, can I go to Diane's house after school tomorrow?

Father

Yes, it is okay. If aajimmy contracted the virus, it would take about three days to show up and spread to someone else, plus he was six feet away from you. But he must stay in his room. I will take him for a test in three days.

Mary

Okay, great! Do not worry; I will have my mask on. I know this virus is for real.

Father

Remember what I told you; every time you visit this family, you come back acting weird and holy. I do not want to hear what you are saying. We do not need God in this house.

Mary

Yes, Dad (she leaves the room)

Mother

I thought the change in Mary could be a good thing.

Father

Do not start! We have never believed or even talked about a god in this house. If she continues, I will stop her from visiting This Jesus-sick family.

Mother

I am just saying this because my co-workers have said the same thing to me. They ask me where we go to church. When I tell them, we do not go to church and do not believe in God. Many of them ask me how I handle the Pandemic without Jesus.

Father

Please do not fall for the nonsense they are telling you. It is all foolish babbling.

(The father leaves the room; the mother is left alone, wiping tears from her eyes.)

Lights out.

Scene Six

(Setting, at Diane's house after school. Diane's parents are home, and Kevin, Mary knock on the door; Diane opens the door)

Mary

Hi Mr. and Mrs. Anderson.

Diane

Please sit, Mary; let me get you something to snack on and water.

Mary

Thanks, I have not eaten since lunch today.

Mother

So, Mary, how is your family?

Mary

They are okay; I think it would be better if I could get them to understand the need for a Savior in their lives, and my brother is being difficult as always, but overall, they are doing well.

Father

Yes, during trials and tribulations, we need someone we can call on at any time.

Mother

Yes, indeed, I do not know what I would do without Him during this Pandemic.

Mary

I cannot get them to see the need for Jesus in their lives. I get angry and frustrated at them when they make fun of me when I tell them that Jesus is the real reason, we celebrate Christmas.

Mother

Mary, sometimes, we must show them Jesus through how we live.

Mary

I know, but it was not hard for me to believe when Diane shared Jesus with me, I did not receive the good news right away. I thought she was different, but she never got angry with me.

Father

Yes, she allowed the Holy Spirit to do His job. Sharing Jesus with someone must be done in love, with the understanding when people reject, it is not us they reject; it is Jesus. Therefore, we cannot take it personally.

Mary

I think taking it personal is my problem; I should not get angry when people do not want to hear about or believe in Jesus.

Mother

Yes, you plant the seed, someone else waters it, and God increases it.

Mary

Okay, I understand; what is taking Diane so long? I am starving.

Mother

Let me check *(she leaves)*

(Kevin walks into the room smiling)

Kevin

Hi, dad! Hi Mary!

Mary

Hi Kevin, how have you been? You are an excellent brother to me; Jimmy can learn a lesson from you.

Kevin

(Reluctantly says) But I am not your brother.

Mary

Well, Diane is like my sister, so this makes you like my brother.

Kevin

Oh, okay *(then he leaves the room, and mother and Diane come in)*

Mother

Diane was baking pizza rolls.

Mary

Thank you, Diane, but I will have to take them to go. My mother just texted me; she is outside.

Diane

Okay, I am sorry it took me so long.

Mary

It's okay; I had an interesting conversation with your parents and learned they are very wise.

Father

To God, be the glory. God bless you. It was our pleasure.

Mother

Yes, it was indeed our pleasure.

Mary

Bye *(she leaves)*

Diane

YES! It worked.

Mother

What do you mean?

Diane

After talking to Mary on the phone yesterday, I knew she needed you and dad's wisdom; I was listening. Thanks, mom, and dad.
(The three of them hugged, sat on the couch, and watched TV)

Lights out.

Scene Seven

(Setting in the home of Mary's family. It has been three days since Jimmy decided not to wear a mask in the mall; Dad walks into his room and sees that he is not there)

Father

(Knocks on Jimmy's door) Jimmy, it is time to get up.

(Dad went back to the table to finish breakfast.)

Mary

Dad, did you have to go back to the hospital last night?

Father

No, why do you ask?

Mary

Because I thought I heard a door closed or I was dreaming.

Father

No, you were dreaming. (He yells) "Jimmy get up; we cannot be late)

Mary

He may have gone to sleep listening to his loud and wild music.

Father

Let me check (he walks into the room, and Jimmy is gone.

Mary

I knew I heard the door close last night.

Mother

Oh, no! Where can he be? Mary, can you call his cellphone?

Mary

I am Mom, but he is not answering.

Father

(Is angry) He is probably at one of his no-good friend's houses.

(*Mom is crying, dad is upset, Mary is praying while her father tells her to stop. Amid the chaos, mother phone rings.*)

Mother

Hello!

Grandmother

Hi Honey, how are you doing?

Mother

Not Good mother, I am frantic right now.

Grandmother

Janice, you are scaring me; what is going on?

Mother

Jimmy is missing!

Grandmother

No, he is not; he is in bed asleep.

Mother

What? Is Jimmy with you?

Grandmother

Yes, he said you dropped him off last night. I hugged and kissed him. I was glad to see him.

Mother

Oh, no, mother, Kevin ran away. He is supposed to take the Covid test because he went to the mall with his friends without wearing a mask.

Grandmother

Oh my, he told me that he was not feeling good. I checked his temperature; he had a low-grade fever.

Mother

(Dropped her phone while screaming no! No!)

Father

Honey, what is wrong?

Mother

Jimmy is with my mother; he went over last night. Mother also said that he had a fever and said that he was not feeling good; she even hugged and kissed him.

Father

This is not good. Honey, grab our mask and let's go and get him. (*They rush out of the house. Mary is left alone; she sat on the chair and started to pray.*)

Lights out.

Scene Eight

(Setting at Mary's parents' home seven days later, Jimmy and grandmother tested positive; grandmother is in critical condition. She is in the hospital. Jimmy is doing better; he is in quarantine in his bedroom, depressed because his grandmother may die because of him; Mary's father is at work.)

Mother

All of this seems like a nightmare, *(with tears in her eyes, she turns to Mary and asks her.)* What is happening? My mother may die; and Jimmy is sick.

Mary

Mom, I do not know what will happen to Jimmy or our grandmother, but Jesus knows; I pray and trust Him.

Mother

How do I pray, Mary?

Mary

I will teach you, but first, you must accept and trust Jesus as your Savior. I called Diane's family; they are praying for us. We will get through this.

(Mother phone rings, a doctor from the hospital who work with her husband told her that he had been admitted; she fell to her knees, screaming and crying. Mary took her mom's phone.)

Mary

My mother just passed out; who is this? What did you tell her?

Doctor

Your father is in the hospital; he is positive for the virus,

Mary

Okay, we are on our way.

Doctor

No, do not! You will not be able to see him. He is on a ventilator.

Mary

Mom, are you okay?

Mother

Yes, but tell me that I am dreaming.

Mary

No, you are not; everything is as real as Jesus is. Our family is in a crisis, just like the world is, and only Jesus can help us.

Mother

Mary, you are calm, and I am a mess.

Mary

Believe me, it is not me, but Jesus, who lives in me. I can do all things through him who strengthens me.

(*Mother phone rang, she was afraid to answer it. She hands the phone to Mary.*)

Mary

Come on and sit down. Mom, grandmother, died.

Mother

(Screams) No! No! (Mary hugs and comforts her mom. By this time, Jimmy comes out of the room wearing his mask. Mary told him the news about their father and Grandmother; he fell to his knees, crying and saying, "What have I done?" Who can help us? Mary calmed him down and got him back in his room. Mom had to take some meds to calm herself. She finally fell asleep.

(Mary's phone should be on speaker so the audience can hear the conversation. She calls Diane to let her know what happened. She asks that Diane's family pray for them. Diane reminded Mary that Christmas is on a Sunday and that they would have service at their church; she says that her family will pray that Mary's family would come. Mary says what better gift one can receive on Christmas Day than Jesus. Diane tells Mary that she will also pray and ask her family. Mary begins to pray.

Lights out.

Scene Nine

(Setting at The Living God Church on December 25, 2020. Grandmother's funeral was one day ago, Dad had a rough time but made I through everything, and Jimmy did too. Mary's and Diane's family finally met before the beginning of the service, practicing social distancing, and wearing masks. Mary excitingly says, well, let us go in and enjoy the Christmas service.)

Pastor

Reads scriptures and prays,

Choir

Does Christmas songs.

Pastor

Preaches a heartfelt sermon about the birth of Jesus and how Jesus is the reason for the season (The Holy Spirit is touching hearts.

Choir

Sings invitation song "Come to Jesus," And the Pastor invites people to Christ.

(Mary's family went down to accept Jesus as Savior; Ms. Johnson, Mary's teacher, and Mr. Shaw, the principal, along with other people, went also; the Pastor led the lost to Christ in a Prayer of repentance, forgiveness, and acceptance of Jesus Christ. Everybody is rejoicing now as the Pastor Thank God for the new souls who gave their lives to Christ, and they praise God)

Lights out.

———— ∞ ————

Scene Ten (Final)

(Setting back at Mary's house)

Father

Mary, what an incredible feeling I have. Please find it in your heart to forgive me for my attitude against you when you spoke of Jesus.

Mother

Yes, me too.

Jimmy

Yes, Mary, I am so sorry. Mom and Dad, please forgive me for acting immaturely. Because of me, grandmother is dead, and dad almost died, and I am so sorry. (Jimmy cries)

Mary

It is okay; God has already forgiven all of you. He has given you all a new start; He loves all of us. I thank God for prayer, prayer works.

Mother

My mother is ok; she is in Heaven with Jesus. She taught us about Jesus; I chose not to accept Him.

Jimmy

Thank you, God, for forgiving me; thank you for the best gift one could ever receive.

Mary

Yes, Jimmy, and it is free, then she says, "Who is the reason for the season?

All

Jesus is the reason for the season.

Mother

Now that we know the real reason for the season, let us open presents.

(They sat around the tree opening gifts as the lights went out.

IT TOUCHED MY HEART
(A TRUE STORY)

Once, when I was teaching Children's Church in 2001, I met a little girl who had never attended church. Oh, how it touched me as I wondered how that could be. She told me she had never heard of Christ. Tears covered my eyes as I stood there, wondering why. I knew at that moment she needed to hear about our Savior.

As I told her about how Christ died on the cross for our sins, her eyes lit up. She was amazed at what was being said. She wanted to hear more. I was excited as I told the story. The little girl was pleased that I, along with the other kids in children's church, would take the time to tell her how and why Christ came to Earth. I told her about His amazing birth. Then I asked her if she knew about sin. She had a confused look on her little face. I thought oh my, today she is in the right place.

I had all the kids explain to her the meaning of sin. Afterward, she had a clear understanding. She also understood that if she believed in Christ, He would forgive all her sins.

I asked her if she was familiar with Heaven and Hell. I saw another puzzled look on her face, and all the kids raised their hands to be the first to tell her about the beautiful kingdom of God and how awful Satan's home in Hell would be for unbelievers.

By the time service ended, she knew exactly who Christ was and why He came to Earth. The children and I felt blessed because we had done what

Christ commanded us to do. You see, Christ wants us to go out and share the good news.

God was smiling on my class of little warriors for Jesus. That Sunday morning was a blessing for the little girl who visited our class and me and the other children. They got a chance to see that there are people in the world who haven't heard about God's goodness, grace, and mercy. They learned how important it is to share Christ and His Word with those who may not know Him.

May God continue to bless the little girl who visited our class that Sunday and continue to bless my class as they grow in the knowledge of our Lord Jesus Christ.

FATHER, PLEASE BLESS THIS BOOK

Father God, who art in Heaven, I thank you for inspiring and giving me the wisdom, knowledge, and understanding to write this book. Father, I prayed and asked you to reveal your will and purpose for my life. You listened and answered, and I obeyed. This book is your will, and I ask you to please bless it.

Father God, I thank you for revealing part of your will to me. I will continue to pray and ask for more of your will in my life because I know that you have a lot of work for me to do to further your kingdom. Now, Father, I pray this book will reach many people and touch many hearts. I also pray that through this book, many lives will be saved. I pray that many will ask, "What must I do to be saved?" Father, you know my heart, and my purpose for writing this book.

Father God, once again, I thank you for inspiring me to write this book to share the good news about our Lord and Savior. Thank you for blessing this book in Jesus' name. Amen.

Printed in the United States
by Baker & Taylor Publisher Services